MARKS & SPENCER

CW01625421

tenminute yoga

Christina Brown

Marks and Spencer p.l.c.
PO Box 3339, Chester CH99 9QS

www.marksandspencer.com

ISBN: 1-84461-016-0

Printed in China

Produced by the
BRIDGEWATER BOOK COMPANY LTD

Photographer: Mike Hemsley at Walter Gardiner

Picture acknowledgements: The publishers would like to thank the following for the use of photographs: Getty Images 5 (Darren Robb), 8 (Antony Nagelmann), 15 (Marc Romanelli); Corbis Images 10tl (Lee White), 10bl (Matthew Alan), 19 (Duomo); Guy Rycart 9.

Contents

Introduction

Yoga is not merely a series of exercises that simultaneously energize and relax the body, it is a means of harmonizing the mind, body and spirit. As such, it is a great tool of transformation. In the *chitta-vrtti*, a text that codifies the subject, yoga is defined as *chitta-vrtti-nirohdah*, the cessation of the fluctuations of the mind. Yoga is actually a state of being rather than an exercise or a physical posture.

The aim of yoga is to separate the spirit within from the physical body which acts as its vessel. As the yoga practitioner seeks control over the mind, the thoughts are stilled and the yogi's essential purity is regained. This neutralization of the turnings of thought occurs in a trance-like state known as *samadhi*.

Asana, the use of physical postures, is the practice most commonly equated with yoga in the west. Asana helps to open and prepare the body for the long hours of meditation necessary to reach this goal. It also alters the subtle energies of the body, clearing the path for the experience of higher states.

The word yoga originates from the Sanskrit *yug*, meaning 'to yoke'. Yoking, or harnessing energies, implies effort, and a goal such as samadhi certainly requires discipline. Though the starting point for many people is a few yoga postures, hatha yoga, sometimes referred to as the 'yoga of force', also includes codes of moral conduct, asanas, concentration, breathing practices and meditation. These are the tools to achieve union with the cosmic universal power and the state of yoga.

Self-realization and entering samadhi are lofty goals indeed. More realistically, yoga practice has a lot to offer us in the 21st century. Yug is also translated as 'to link or unify'. By connecting thought, breath and posture, yoga aligns the mental, physical and emotional bodies. Yoga practice offers a chance to return to the integrated self and experience the truth of who we are. In experiencing these mini self-realizations, we get a glimpse of our essential purity. It is like remembering who we really are, but, caught up in the whirlwind of life, we had forgotten.

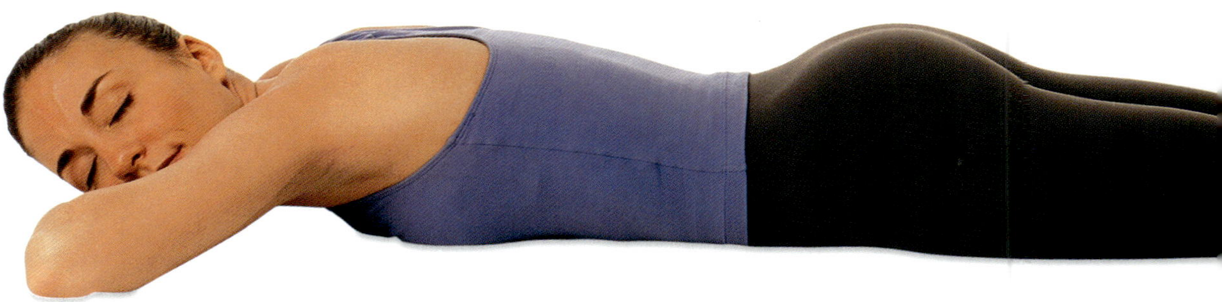

Every yoga practice is a small reversal of consciousness. Yoga teaches us to quieten the mind and observe the present moment. In a refreshing way, our minds are jolted out of our everyday way of thinking. It teaches patience and humbleness in the face of difficulty. We learn to respond to challenges. Yoga expands the heart and gives a sense of wholeness and peace.

Ideally yoga should be practised daily—ten minutes is all it can take for the relaxing powers of yoga to help your mind and body escape from the stresses and strains of a busy, modern life.

Yoga practice works on all elements of our experience, bringing our mind, body and spirit into harmony. Ultimately, it can help to unite us with the energy of the universe.

By practising ten minutes of yoga in the morning and evening, or taking time out from your working day, you can focus your mind and relax your body.

This book contains a selection of postures for you to undertake, as well as concentration, meditation and breathing exercises. You should aim to practice a range of different exercises: try pairing one or more asanas in the morning with some meditation or relaxation in the evening. And although these exercises are great for short sessions, when time allows try an occasional longer session by combining different exercises.

1 Background and Basics

We are often not fully aware of how we hold ourselves, but bad habits can distort our posture. Sometimes a tight area of the body is compensating for a weaker area, and this gradually changes the way we carry ourselves, pulling the body out of line. Even our bones can change shape over time. Bone cells are constantly broken down and new cells are created where they will best sustain the force of the most common daily impacts.

Yoga helps us to bring the body back to its natural alignment. As we practise, we can strengthen weaker zones so that areas of higher tension will be able to lessen their protective holding. Ten-minute yoga can help achieve this. However, to help undo less than optimal holding patterns, you should attend regular classes with an experienced teacher who can work on your alignment.

asana and *alignment*

Yoga postures are based on ancient geometrical shapes. When performed with attention to alignment, these asanas redesign the body. Muscles are trained to lengthen out of their habitual tense, shortened holding patterns.

Asanas assist the rhythmic pulsations of the body. The circulation of blood and cerebrospinal fluid, the digestion, excretion, lymphatic drainage and all the organs require rhythmic pulsation to maintain good health. By freeing up the body for these natural pulsations to take place, yoga postures aid good health. Practising yoga postures is like giving yourself a massage, working not just the muscles, but the deeper tissues and internal organs, too. Asanas are a great form of do-it-yourself preventive medicine.

Asanas work on more than just a physical level. They take the intelligence normally considered to reside in the mind and spread it throughout the entire body. Consciousness can reach everywhere. In the perfect asana, the mind is so engrossed that there is no room for other thoughts to arise. Asanas have psycho-spiritual effects. They influence the emotions and express qualities of the heart.

By aligning the outer body, asanas improve the energy flow in the inner body. Asanas help keep, build and control the vital force, the *prana*.

One of the most common mental blocks for a beginner is the belief that they are not flexible enough for yoga. However, if you perform a pose with honest effort and correct alignment, you will achieve a result similar to that of someone who seems more flexible. Do not despair about your lack of flexibility; the true measure of your asana is being mentally present – aware of the whole body – and having a calm and steady breath.

Yoga postures work on the internal organs as well as the muscles and bones. Twists like this one give the abdominal organs a good stretch.

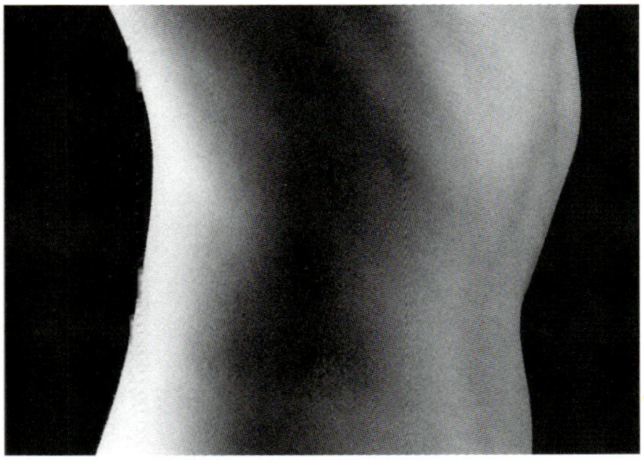

Over time, regular yoga practice will help to deepen your breathing and correct distortions in posture.

Breathing

The mind and breath are interrelated; an alteration in one affects the other. By nature, the breath is more constant than the mind. The mind can multiply in ways the breath cannot. Focusing on the breath in asana practice helps to calm the consciousness. For this reason, never force the breath. Inhalations and exhalations are like waves breaking on the shore. Keep them even to develop evenness in the mind.

Conscious breathing in a pose will deepen your awareness and keep your mind free of distraction. The breath is your monitor of how you are doing in the pose. When the breath is perfectly steady, your asana is closer to being perfected.

Breathe through the nose not the mouth, so the air is filtered and warmed. Perform asanas with Ujjayi breathing (see page 110). As a general rule inhale when you come up out of a pose, when raising the arms, and during movements that expand the chest such as bending backwards. Exhale when moving downwards, lowering the arms or bending forwards.

Good steady breathing is a vital aspect of yoga practice. It helps you to concentrate and also gives you the energy to hold a posture for longer.

awareness, focus and *being present*

When an asana is performed with full awareness, it develops into something far greater than just an element within a fitness regime. Work with integrity. Become absorbed in the subtle sensations of the body. From observing your hamstring in a forward bend, for example, spread your awareness to the whole leg, then to your lower back. Without forgetting the original point, radiate your awareness out until it touches the entire body. The essence of yoga is not about twisting yourself into complicated pretzel shapes. Doing the most difficult-looking asanas is not the goal. Rather, mastery of an asana comes when a perfect awareness of the whole body and breath can be maintained.

Working consciously focuses your attention right at the present moment. You may spend one minute in a particular posture. During this minute, you let go, observe and refine, seeking the still point, the epicentre of consciousness. During yoga, these minutes link together. If each asana is a pearl, an asana practice forms a beautiful necklace. Over time, this 'one minute' focus can extend into your day-to-day life. Yoga is practising being in the 'now'. Give attention to the breath, which will bring you back to the present. When you are fully in the present, worries about the future dissipate. Stress floats away when you can release the past and let go of concerns for the future.

Effort

Fully engaging a muscle helps to bring the mind right to that area. Engaging a muscle group increases awareness and is good practice for concentration and being in the now. When the muscles are engaged, the mind is engaged – one reason why asanas have transformative power. The effort required teaches discipline and is rewarding.

For beginners, holding a posture might require 90 per cent effort. It is hard to feel the surrender and release that is the other 10 per cent. With time and dedication this percentage shifts. The asana becomes more comfortable and feels more rewarding, as the effort it demands falls to 80 per cent, then 70 per cent and so on. Experiencing the freedom in the pose by yielding into it is sweetly satisfying.

There needs to be a balance between effort and surrender. If you don't extend yourself fully, the practice will be too easy, and your attention will wander. When you overextend yourself, it becomes so difficult that your practice will not be joyful. Practising with effort doesn't mean using excess force. Frowning, clenching your jaw or holding your breath are signs to back off. If you feel competitive, smile kindly upon yourself, and let go of your over-ambitiousness. Your practice is a metaphor for life. Delight in it.

Surrender

Life experiences build up like layers and are stored in the cellular memory of our bodies. Yoga helps us to strip off the superfluous emotional overlays that hold us back. There is a sense of freedom and peace within when we start to discover our true essence.

We are accustomed to the concept of using effort to get somewhere. Letting go in order to achieve something might seem strange. Yoga uses effort – doing – to aid surrender – undoing. With yoga you can often do more by undoing. As you release the air from your lungs, release the tension in the body. Don't force it. To extend further, yield with each exhalation. Use rhythm to help you relax into the poses. If you have difficulty getting a sensation of release in a pose, use external movement. Move in and out of the pose with a rhythmic flow several times before holding the pose steady.

Finding the Edge

Learning to extend yourself to the limit requires experimentation to find just where the frontier lies. It changes daily, so you have to rediscover the edge in each pose of every practice. Metaphysically, reaching your edge and nudging your boundaries challenge your perception of where you are at. Yoga asanas are a controlled means of exposing yourself to a difficult situation. They are meant to try you. They offer practice at not being stressed in stressful conditions.

A single posture will have many edges. As you arrive at the first one, stay steady and breathe for a while. Have patience. Wait for the posture to let you in. When it does, enter respectfully. Again hold and breathe at this new edge, waiting for the invitation from your body to enter.

As you approach your 'edge', distinguish between discomfort and pain. On the road to strength, flexibility and focus, mental and physical unease inevitably arises. Discomfort is just resistance of the body or mind. Don't fight physical unease, but soften into it. For mental unease, become absorbed by the breath to return to the present.

Pain is more acute than discomfort. Pain in a pose means you have approached your edge too fast and gone too far or that you are improperly aligned. Pain in the muscles or joints should not be ignored because it can lead to injury. Come out of the pose and examine your alignment. Consult a teacher if necessary. In time you will become more body aware and better able to listen to feedback from your body.

From breathing exercises to asanas, yoga is a balance between effort and letting go.

grounding

If you want one part of your body to rise up, you must anchor another part down. Each pose has an anchor point. Working from this base teaches you how to extend yourself, while not losing yourself. When no attention is given to grounding, yoga poses risk turning into a series of mere stretches.

Often less flexible people practise better yoga than very flexible ones, because stiffer bodied people have more intuitive experience about anchoring and working from their base. Very 'stretchy' people sometimes find it hard to learn to anchor themselves. A certain amount of stability is always needed, both in the poses and in life itself. The earth supports, shelters and feeds us, yet sometimes we lose our sense of connection with it. Re-centre, find your balance and extend yourself to your limit without losing awareness of what is always there to support you.

Resting

Nobody would expect a car driven continuously, at high speed, not to deteriorate. Yet many of us expect this from our bodies. Relaxation during asana practice allows the body space to give the mind feedback. Awareness and intuition will develop. Until the art of relaxation *within* the postures is developed, rest when necessary between postures. See Relaxation Breaks (pages 40–41) for resting poses.

history and *philosophy*

Many scholars date hatha yoga back to between the ninth and tenth centuries. However, the philosophy and practices were passed down orally before being written down, so it is possible that they are much older than this.

Yoga consists of eight limbs (see page 14), as codified in the *Yoga-sutras*. Written in Sanskrit and attributed to the sage Patanjali, the *Yoga-sutras* is an early yoga text. Patanjali lists the eight limbs in a certain order, starting with moral behaviour and ending with the self-realized state of *samadhi*.

The eight limbs are not steps to be worked on one by one, but branches to be explored several at a time – otherwise we would forever remain at the first precept of the first limb and we'd never move on to practising a single asana.

From a relatively simple beginning of using asanas, yoga sometimes takes you by the hand and leads you on to the higher concepts. You have the support of a force greater than yourself, so it feels like a natural progression to explore some of the other limbs.

The first five limbs are known as the outer limbs. Limbs three, four and five involve the interpenetration of the mind, body and spirit. The last three limbs, the inner limbs, are called the 'wealth of yoga' by Patanjali. It's debatable whether you can 'practise' them or not because they are states of the mind. However, you can make yourself as receptive as possible to them.

Asana practice is one of the eight limbs of yoga. The ultimate aim of all yoga is to achieve samadhi, which is described as a state of absorption with the absolute.

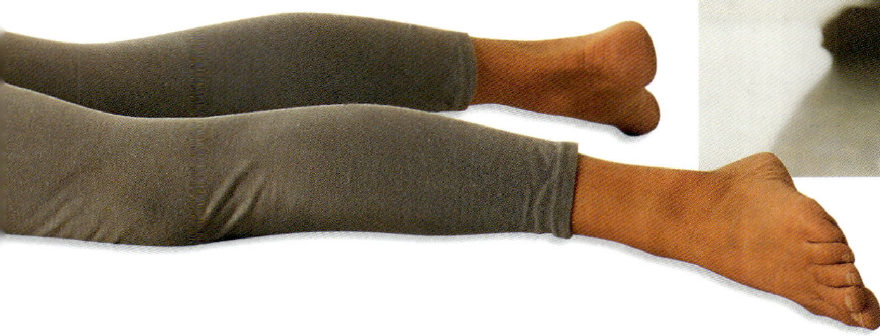

the *eight limbs* of *yoga*

1 *yama* Moral restraints. Five are listed in the Yoga-sutras: non-injury, truthfulness, non-stealing, chastity and non-covetousness.

2 *niyama* Discipline in actions and conduct. Patanjali lists five disciplines: cleanliness, contentment, austerity, continuous learning and surrender to the Divine.

3 *asana* The physical postures of hatha yoga.

4 *pranayama* Breath control to cultivate the vital force within. For more information, see pages 106–113.

5 *pratyahara* Withdrawal of the senses. An example of pratyahara might be when you are so engrossed in watching a movie that you don't hear a fire engine siren outside. The noise is still there but it is not consciously registered; the mind is absorbed so it receives fewer distractions. Often, instead of us controlling the senses, the sense organs become masters over us. Like servants we devote ourselves to satisfying their cravings. On the spiritual path, the mind gradually loses interest in what the senses have to say and pratyahara becomes more natural.

6 *dharana* Mental concentration. This can be developed during asana and pranayama practice. Dharana helps to pave the way to the seventh and eighth limbs.

7 *dhyana* As meditation, dhyana is a one-pointed mental focus.

8 *samadhi* Consciousness is altered in this illuminated state of absorption with the absolute.

At its highest level, yoga can help us to transcend human consciousness. As we practise, we may catch a glimpse of this blissful state of being.

2 Simple Ten-Minute Yoga

There are many different ways to practise yoga. Ideally, you will practise regularly, setting aside enough time to incorporate a range of different postures into each session: forward bends, back bends, twists, inversions and relaxation postures. Over time, you will be able to develop your practice, going into the basic postures more deeply and learning more advanced ones.

You can also use yoga as a feel-good therapy, to give you an instant boost as and when you need it. If you are short of time, it is best to concentrate on simple stretches, forward bends and relaxation postures; ten minutes are all that you need to reap some of the benefits of yoga.

The postures in this section have been specially selected to be done on their own, at any time. These exercises can be done at home, at work or anywhere you have room to stretch out. If you have time, end with a relaxation pose or try one of the relaxation breaks described in Chapter 3.

starting the *practice*

These guidelines will help you get the most from your practice session. Remember that in yoga it is important to focus on the journey, rather than just the destination.

Yoga makes energy available to the cells for repair and detoxification. Avoid diverting this energy to the digestion. Don't practise on a full stomach. Leave four hours after a large meal before practising and wait half an hour after your practice before eating. If possible, avoid drinking water during the practice.

A simple forward bend can be a wonderful way of releasing tension.

A balanced practice will include a forward bend, side bend, back bend, twist, balance, inversion and a final relaxation. Always include a pose that makes you feel good about your practice, and include one you don't like so much, as that one is probably what you need most.

When you are short of time, practising fewer poses with full attention is preferable to rushing through many poses. Choose simple poses and focus on your breathing and mental awareness. In this way, you can reap the rewards of yoga in as little as ten minutes. Practising twice a week is a good start. Three times a week heralds a deeper level of transformation. If your practice is intense, rest one day a week.

Though the idea is lovely, practising in direct sunlight tends to be fatiguing. Choose a warm spot, with a clean, level surface. A cushioned surface is nice for some of the floor poses. Sticky mats offer cushioning and will prevent slipping in the standing postures. Choose clothes that let you stretch and that you feel good in.

Women should take things easy during the initial days of menstruation. Avoid inverted postures, strong back bends and twists because they can affect the flow of blood. Practise restorative poses, such as forward bends and relaxation.

While yoga has helped the pregnancies and labours of countless women, the first three months of pregnancy is not a safe time to begin. Many poses need to be modified so it's best to attend specialized classes during the second and third trimesters.

If you are suffering from a health condition or have an injury, seek guidance from an experienced yoga teacher or a health practitioner who understands yoga. It is inadvisable to practise asana or pranayama if you have a fever.

If you have ten minutes to spare, take the time to do some breathing practice. All you need is a quiet space to sit in.

awareness of the breath

When you practise yoga you are dedicating some time to yourself. Regular ten-minute sessions can improve your physical and mental well-being. Unplug the telephone and close the door on distractions. You might like to light a candle to honour the light you carry within. With regard to the outside energies greater than yourself, you could offer a prayer or chant. Begin by lying down or sitting in order to access the stillness within. Quieten the mind and observe the moment by focusing on your breath.

1 Lie on your left side with your knees bent. Reach your arms straight out in front, palms together. Gaze at your right thumb and, inhaling, take your right arm up into the air until your fingers point straight up to the sky.

exploreyoga

When you start practising yoga, it can be very hard to focus. If you notice that your thoughts have wandered, pause for a moment and bring your attention to your breathing. Feel the inhalation and the exhalation of air through your nostrils or notice the rise and fall of your chest.

2 Exhale as you take your right arm toward the floor behind you. If you are flexible in the shoulders, the back of your hand may go all the way to the floor. On your next inhalation, bring your arm back up to halfway, still following its path with your eyes. Check you are not slumping into your right shoulder, but reaching away with your whole arm. Exhale it down to join the palms together.

Continue for six more rounds. As your breath is slow and constant, so is your rate of movement. Time the movement to follow the breath. Your fingers point skyward with the end of each inhalation. Your opening out and returning to base coincide with the end of the exhalation.

3 As you open out on the sixth round, let the back of your hand rest on the floor. Hold this position and take six deep breaths. Bring more of the right side of your back into contact with the floor as you deepen the twist in your waist. Reach your right arm away and feel your shoulders widen. This position gives a gentle opening of the chest. Don't rush on to the next inhalation between breaths, but allow it to arise naturally. As you lie quietly, each exhalation brings softening and release.

4 When you are ready to repeat on the right side, keep the arms spread apart and inhale as you bring your legs up to centre and over to lie on your right side.

biralasana

cat pose

This exercise brings awareness and flexibility to the entire length of the spine. Channelling the breath into movement is centring and helps to keep the flow of the breath constant.

2 Inhale and look up, and curve your back downwards. Accentuate the curve in the small of your back and raise your tailbone. Keep the back of your neck long as you gaze upwards. Without slumping into the shoulders, move your breastbone forward and up.

1 Start on all fours. Have your knees under your hips and your hands under your shoulders. Position the hands so both middle fingers stretch straight forward. Gaze at the floor between your hands in this neutral position.

3 As you exhale, tuck your pelvis under, and round your back. Your upper back arches naturally in this way, but try to make the lower back curve in the same way. As you press each vertebra up to the sky, feel your shoulder blades spread apart and earth your palms by pressing them evenly into the floor. As you finish your exhalation, move your chin towards your breastbone. Repeat ten more rounds, arching and curving in time with your breath. Maintain perfect awareness so that you curve deeper each time. To deepen the pose, walk the hands in 8cm (3in) to accentuate the curves.

tip

Focus on a single vertebra for several rounds. Mentally go inside to feel how it works.

roll downs

Working through this sequence will allow you to learn about how 'undoing', rather than active 'doing', can deepen a pose.

1 Stand tall with your feet hip-width apart. Relax your shoulders. You are going to take several breaths to fold forwards by rolling down the spine.

2 As you exhale, drop your head forward. Feel how the shoulders want to follow. Release your knees so they bend slightly. On your next exhalation let the shoulders go and the upper back round more. Your arms hang down vertically, dangling passively out of their sockets. Continue exhaling and rolling down the back in stages, leading with the head. Your knees will bend more the further you roll down. Take as many breaths as you need to release all the way down.

3 Even though your legs are working, your upper body is dangling, hanging out of the hips. Bring a rag-doll quality to the upper body. Move your awareness to the shoulders and relax them fully so the arms hang loose. Relax the back of the neck so the crown of the head is the closest part of the head to the floor.

4 Take several rounds of breathing, observing the movements intrinsically related to the breath. As you inhale there is a lifting energy in the core of the body. If your knees are bent enough, a small lengthening occurs from pubic bone to throat. As you exhale your ribs will fall closer to your thighs.

5 When it's time to come up, keep the knees bent and, over several breaths, roll up slowly through the spine, as if you are stacking each vertebra on top of the last. Exhale as you release your arms down to your sides.

sukhasana forward fold

cross-legged forward fold

Sukha means content or happy. Spending a few minutes letting yourself soften into this pose is a centring way to start your practice or to help yourself to relax.

1 Sit in a simple cross-legged position. To work deeper into the hips, slide your heels away from each other so they rest under the knees. Then take the feet forward so the shins are in a horizontal line.

2 Become aware of the sitting bones in contact with the floor. This base will act as your anchor as you stretch forward. Place your fingertips on the floor just in front of your legs. Now lengthen the sides of the torso from hips to armpits. Use several breaths to let this releasing take place. When you feel ready, creep the hands away. Work with your breath as you take one or two minutes to slide the hands forward in stages. Only drop your forehead down to the floor if you are very flexible and your front ribs come to lie on your legs. Then repeat with the legs crossed the other way.

explore*yoga*

Don't become mentally lazy. Stay aware throughout. If you are performing the pose automatically, you might just stay at the point you initially reached. When you hold a pose for a longer period, you will often find you can go much deeper and extend yourself to a new edge.

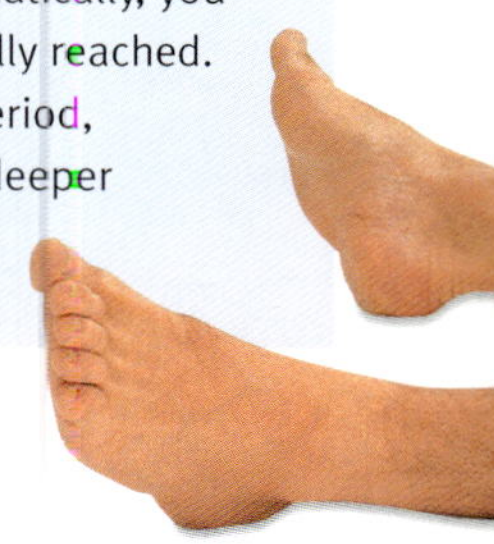

revitalizing *relaxation*

To make a breathing bed, fold one to three blankets so they are 20cm (8in) wide and longer than your torso. Lie over them with your buttocks on the floor and legs a little apart. The more blankets you use, the more the chest will feel it is opening, so experiment with what feels best for you. Use another blanket as a pillow so that the head is higher than the chest. Take your legs apart and let your arms rest out to the sides.

Lie on your back. Lift your head for a moment and look down your body to make sure you are perfectly symmetrical. If not, change your position. After checking that you feel completely comfortable, begin to breathe deeply and rhythmically. As you inhale, visualize prana (energy) being drawn in through the nostrils down to your solar plexus. As you exhale, feel it swirl around your centre. With each inhalation, draw this pranic energy down to the solar plexus, feeling the spiral becoming larger and larger until it fills up the whole torso. Let each long, deep inhalation draw in more prana. While you are giving yourself this gift of vibrant energy, remember to keep the exhalations slow and steady. The full exhalation empties the lungs, allowing you to inhale this revitalizing force deeply and consciously.

From the centre of the torso, feel the spiral enlarge to cover the whole body. The outer part of the spiral reaches to circle over the head, fingertips and toes, encompassing your entire body. Let yourself become the breath. With this positive energy you become enthusiastic about life and your tasks. You gain the energy to fulfil them. Stay in this position for as long as you feel the need.

When it is time to 'awaken', start by moving your body and stretching a little. Allow yourself to feel so revitalized that the eyes blink open, powered by the energy within.

explore*yoga*

You can also visualize yourself being surrounded by glowing white light. This is a good exercise to try if you want to stay true to your inner self and protect yourself from being harmed or drained by others.

surya namaskar

sun salutation

The flowing folding and unfolding of sun salutation is a great way to start the day. A single breath carries you into each pose. Start with three rounds and build to six, offering each one up like a prayer. End your session with five minutes' relaxation.

1

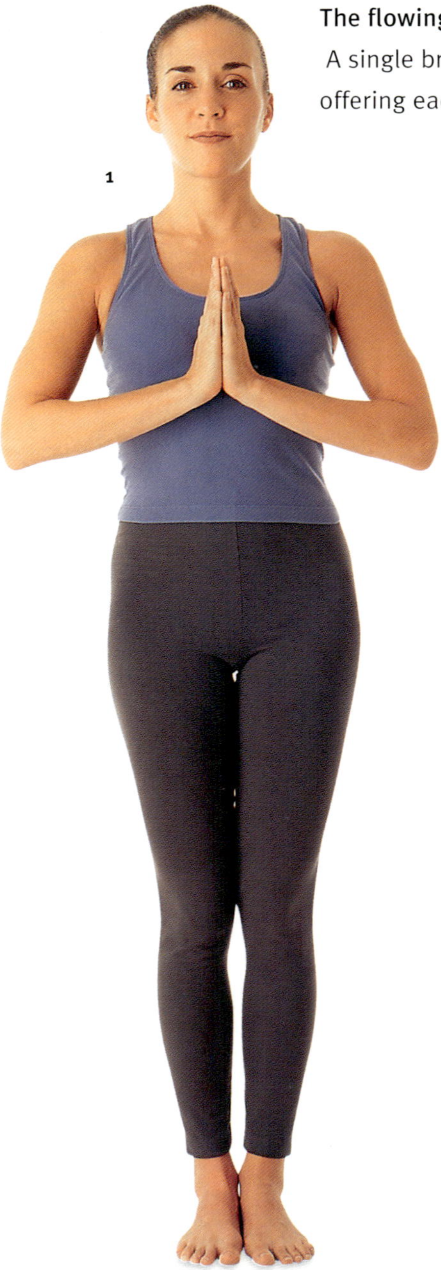

2

3

1 Stand in Samasthiti pose (see page 46), hands in prayer.

2 Inhale and take your arms overhead. Ground through your feet, lift up your torso out of your hips and make a gentle back bend.

3 Exhale and fold forwards to Uttanasana (see pages 52–53). Bend your knees, if necessary, to bring your finger tips or even palms to the floor.

4 Inhale and look forward as you step your right leg back to lunge, knee to the floor. Press your fingertips to the floor as you lift your chest away from your left thigh.

5 Exhale and step your left leg back so your body makes a straight line from heels to head.

6 Inhale as you bring your knees to the floor. Then exhale as you lower your chest and chin to touch the floor.

tip

Vary your sun salutation by holding each pose for three breaths. This gives you time to feel your way into the pose and deepen it.

4

5

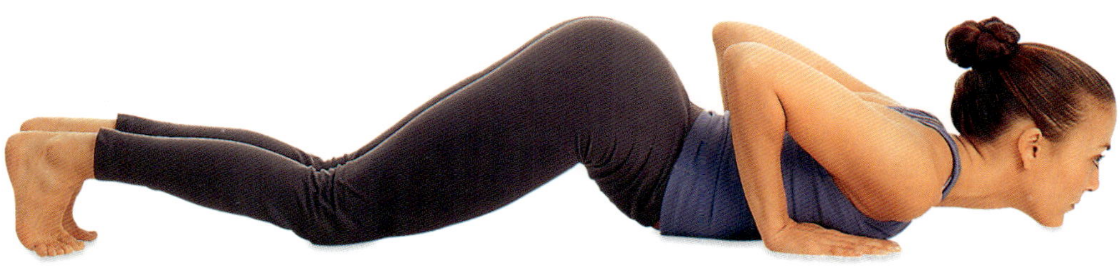

6

7

7 Inhale as you roll up to cobra pose (see pages 62–63).

8 Exhale to downward-facing dog (see pages 74–75).

9 Inhale and step your right leg forward.

8

9

10

11

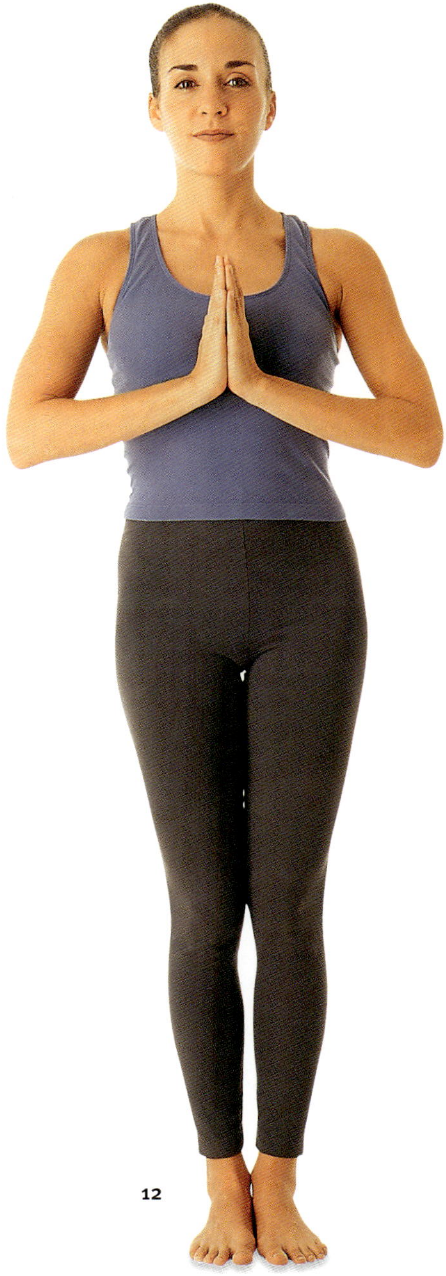

12

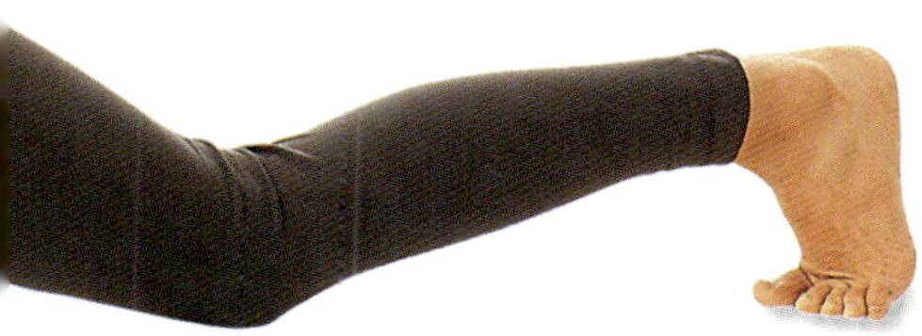

10 Exhale, step your left leg forward and fold into Uttanasana (see pages 52–53).

11 Inhale and firm your front thigh and abdominal muscles as you stand to reach your arms overhead.

12 Exhale to Samasthithi (see page 46). Inhale and repeat on the left side.

ten-minute *yoga* on a *chair*

These make great office exercises and they take only a few minutes to do. If you are at work, shut the door and take your phone off the hook to give yourself the best chance for full mental relaxation.

Back Bend

Different chairs give you stretches of various intensities at different points along the spine; experiment with a few to find the best one for you. The chair back should be below or level with the lower part of your shoulder blades. If your chair is high-backed, sit on telephone books to raise your seat. Lift out of your hips and lean back over your chair. Let your head move back as you stretch your chin away.

Take the arms overhead and stretch them away like two rays of energy to expand the backbend and make this stretch more invigorating. Take care that you do not slump – keep each vertebra actively lifting away from the one below it. Take five to ten chest-opening breaths.

Centring

Sit comfortably on your chair. Have your feet well anchored to the ground. Bring the backs of your hands to your thighs. Sit with your back erect so you are not leaning against the backrest. Let your arms and shoulders relax and have your chin parallel to the floor. With each inhalation observe the expansion of the abdomen, ribs and chest. The whole torso is alive with the gentle pulsation of the breath. Even the back of the body opens up, then softens inwards rhythmically. Raise the inhalation from the back of the waist, upward. Each time you exhale feel the natural, passive release. As all heavy thoughts float away, the head will lighten until it feels like it's floating happily on the top of your spine.

The more you practise this pose, the quicker you will be able to re-centre yourself. Do it whenever you can throughout the day, letting tensions drift away as you return to your true, peaceful inner self.

Twist

Sit with your left hip to the back of the chair. Have your knees and feet hip-width apart. Rest your feet on a support if they don't easily meet the ground. Raise your arms straight up in the air. Let your torso rise out of your hips. Keep this lift as you twist around to the left and hold the back of the chair. Work from a steady base by keeping your hips and knees level. Follow the principles described on page 91 to twist progressively up the spine. Stay for ten breaths before changing sides.

Relaxing Forward Bend

Sit on the chair with your feet body-width apart. If your feet don't touch the floor easily, place a telephone directory underfoot. Fold forwards, keeping your back flat, and lay your ribs on your thighs. Like a rag doll, your arms just hang out of their sockets, backs of the hands on the floor, fingers softly curled. Your upper body grows heavier. Completely let go of your head and shoulders so they release down towards the floor. Let any worries drop away. Now deepen the breath, so the front of your torso expands into the thighs and the space between them. Follow your exhalation for its entire length and observe how it lengthens effortlessly. Stay like this one to five minutes before slowly coming up.

Palming

Refresh with your own portable eyebag. Rub your hands together so the friction builds heat. Place your elbows on a desk or table and rest your head into your hands, palms over your closed eyes. Lean forward to apply a gentle pressure to your eyelids. Withdraw into yourself and observe the wave-like rhythm of your breath.

Shoulder Stretches

The arm positions of Gomukhasana (see page 84), and Garudasana (see pages 56–57) can easily be practised in a chair and are great for those working in offices.

explore*yoga*

Stretch your body at any time, using walls or the poles at bus stops, or by grasping doorways and hanging forwards to open the chest. While watching TV, sit on the floor for ten minutes and use the sofa as a support for Baddha Konasana (see page 81).

3 Relaxation

The role of deep relaxation should never been underestimated. Yoga postures strengthen the prana, the vital life force which heals and revitalizes the mind and body. During yoga relaxation, the prana built up by your asana practice is consolidated, so that it is kept within the body rather than being dispersed and lost. In some ways relaxation is the most important part of the yoga practice. It should never be skipped, even if you are doing just a ten-minute session.

From the outside, deep relaxation looks as easy as taking a nap. In fact, many people find it the most difficult aspect of yoga. Unlike sleeping, yoga relaxation is a conscious process of learning to undo tension. Each part of the body is brought to mind in turn, then relaxed. Discipline is required to keep the mind alert as the body progressively relaxes. As you develop the ability to stay mentally present throughout your asana practice, full relaxation will come much more easily to you.

getting *comfortable*

It is important to be completely comfortable during the final relaxation. A few modifications may cater to any special needs your body may be experiencing during the practice.

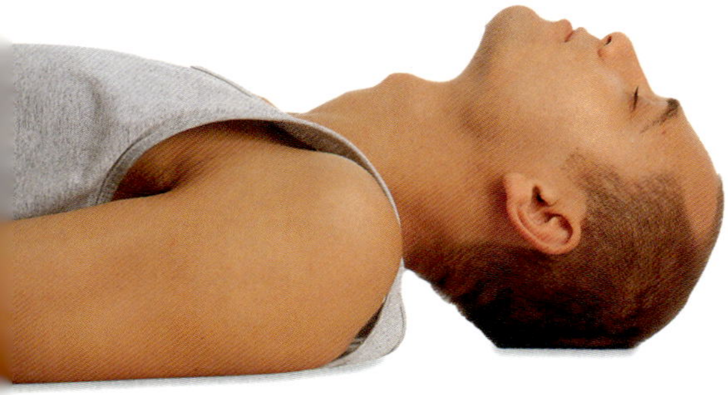

1 Find the best position for your head by having a friend observe you as you lie on your back. Ideally, your chin and forehead will be equal height from the floor. If your chin is higher than your forehead the back of your neck will tend to shorten.

2 Use as many folded blankets as its is necessary to bring your chin and forehead level from the floor. When you have found the right position, your throat won't feel tense or constricted.

yogic thought
Next time you feel tired in the middle of the day, find a quiet space for deep relaxation. Just ten minutes of yoga relaxation can be more refreshing than a nap.

3 Make a neck pillow by folding a blanket three times. Roll up one side of the narrow edge to about half way. Fold in the two corners of the remaining flap to form a triangular shape for your head to rest on. The natural inward curve of the neck should feel completely supported against the firm roll. Lie down to test the height and adjust the size if necessary. Your chin and forehead should be level, and the same height from the floor. Depending on the natural curve in your neck, you might need to raise the level of your head, or lower it by unfolding the triangular flap.

4 When lying flat, the lower back will naturally curve away from the floor. However, If you have an exaggerated curve in the lower back, or a back problem, you might benefit by bending your knees. Place wide pillows or a bolster under your knees to allow the lower back to move a little closer towards the floor.

tip

Keep warm. Feeling cold makes it difficult to relax; the body cools down rapidly in deep relaxation, so cover yourself first with a sheet or blanket.

savasana

corpse pose

While this pose looks like the easiest asana, it is actually one of the hardest to master. Take at least five minutes in relaxation after a short yoga session; longer if you are practising for 30 minutes or more. You can also do this pose by itself – use it as a ten-minute soother whenever you need to relax.

yogic thought

Remember that yoga is not just doing postures, and your yoga practice doesn't have to end here. Integrate yoga into your life by going about your daily life with awareness and consciousness.

1 Lie on your back with your legs a little apart and feet out to the sides. Take your hands a little away from the hips, palms facing upwards, fingers softly curling. Raise your head and look down your body to check the symmetry between left and right sides. Lower your head and close your eyes.

2 Allow five or ten minutes to soften each part of your body systematically. Sweep your mind over your body from toes and fingertips to the crown of your head. Don't skip anywhere; become aware of each part, and where there is tension, relax it.

3 Finally, bring your awareness to your face and scalp. Relax your mouth by slightly separating bottom lip from top. Take your tongue away from the roof of your mouth and let it float in the centre. Feel your jaw muscles release. As your eyes relax, your eyeballs will seem to sink deeper into their sockets. Release any holding in your eyelids, your forehead. Soften the skin on your face so it feels as though any lines smooth out and disappear.

4 Now that each part of your body is relaxed, mentally commit yourself to staying perfectly still until your relaxation is complete. As with meditation (see pages 116–117), any outer movement will distract you from your inner world. Keep your mind alert and observe the sensations in the body. As your body progressively lets go, give permission for your emotional body to let go, too. Each exhalation brings a deeper relaxation, so the body feels heavier, as if sinking into warm earth. Each inhalation distributes life force to all the cells in the body. Should your mind wander, gently bring it back to the delicate breath. The more you focus mentally on this process, the deeper you will go.

5 When it's time to come out of Savasana, deepen your breath. Each inhalation fills your body with energy until your eyes energized from inside, naturally want to blink open. Take one arm overhead and roll over to curl up on that side. When you are ready, slowly come up to sit quietly.

tip

Use visualization to fill your body with positive energy. Choose a colour which connotes a healing energy such as green or rose-pink. With each breath, inhale this coloured light into your centre. Each inhalation will brighten this light, while each exhalation increases its density at your core, until it begins to expand outwards to fill the rest of your body. Pay particular attention to filling up any weaker area with this positive energy. Inhale your whole body so full with the light that it spills over the edges and floats around you. Know that when you come out of the relaxation, you will always have your breath as a tool, any time you need it.

deepen it

Exaggerating muscle tension raises your level of awareness. Work through the body, tensing each section of the body for a few seconds, to allow a deeper surrendering into the relaxation.

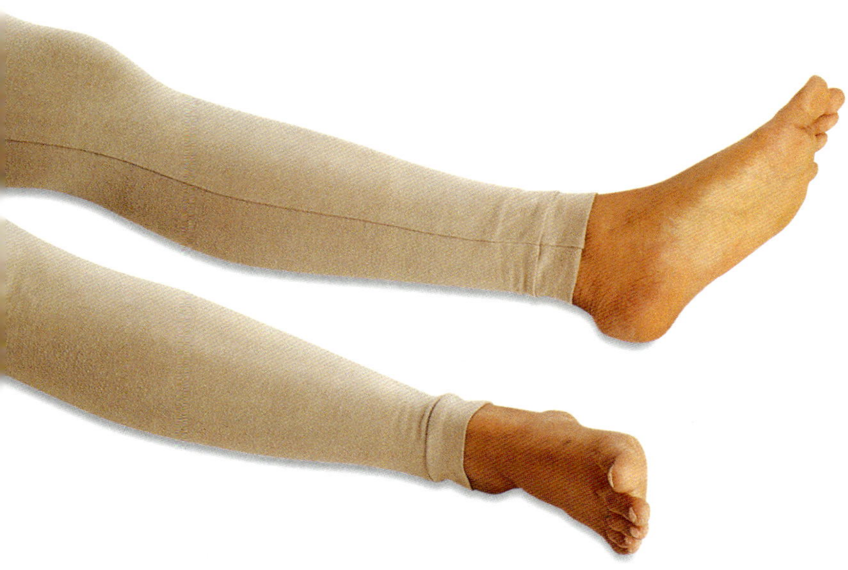

relaxation breaks

Use these poses to relax and renew whenever you wish during your practice, or for a quick ten-minute break at any time during your day. Sprinkling your asana practice with these poses gives you a quiet receptive space to receive feedback from your body.

Balasana – Child Pose

Sit on your heels with your knees together. Fold forward to lay your torso on your thighs. Bring your forehead to the floor and rest the backs of your arms on the floor. Soften your shoulders, close your eyes and follow your breath.

A variation is to keep your big toes together as you spread your knees apart and stretch your arms forward along the floor. If you have high blood pressure or if your buttocks don't release down close to your heels, modify the pose: stack two fists up and rest your forehead on them.

Makrasana – Crocodile Pose

Gentle pressure on the forehead relaxes the frontal lobe of the brain, which helps quieten and soothe your mind.

Lie on your front with your feet comfortably wide apart. Turn your toes outwards. Take your elbows to the floor about 15cm (6in) in front of your shoulders. Grasp each arm above the elbow and rest your forehead down on your forearms, neck soft and relaxed. With your chest on the floor, your upper body is in a gentle back bend. If necessary, adjust the elbows forward or back to find the most comfortable position. Tune into the soothing sensation of the abdomen expanding and pressing into the floor with each breath.

Viparita Karani – Restorative Inversion

Viparita Karani literally means against the grain, as the normal flow of the circulation in the legs is altered. Do it daily for ten minutes if you have varicose veins, or do the pose without the blankets as a quick relaxer.

Fold two or three blankets four times and place them 8cm (3in) out from the wall. Sit on them, side on, with one hip to the wall. Support yourself with your hands, as you swivel around to lay yourself down. Straighten your legs up the wall. Have your buttocks as close to the wall as possible. Lift your head up to make sure your trunk is perpendicular to the wall. Have your arms a little out from your sides, palms up. Close your eyes.

tip

Uttanasana (see pages 52–53) and Adho Mukha Svanasana (see pages 74–75) are useful poses for re-centring.

4 Standing Poses

Standing poses give us the opportunity to explore our connection with the earth beneath our feet. They teach us how to maintain a stable base while extending ourselves upwards.

Ten-minute routines of standing poses can help to develop strength, stamina, focus and stability. They allow you to activate your muscles and joints relatively easily, and encourage control over the entire body. Though the leg muscles need to be worked in standing poses, do not allow the firmness in the muscles to make them static, or to make your breath irregular. Bring an element of softness and release to this firmness, too.

Wide stance poses give greater spinal extension than postures in which the feet are close together, but they also make it more difficult to balance. The mental focus needed to keep your balance helps to develop awareness and concentration, which benefits the rest of your practice.

You should avoid standing postures if you have acute asthma, colitis or cardiac problems.

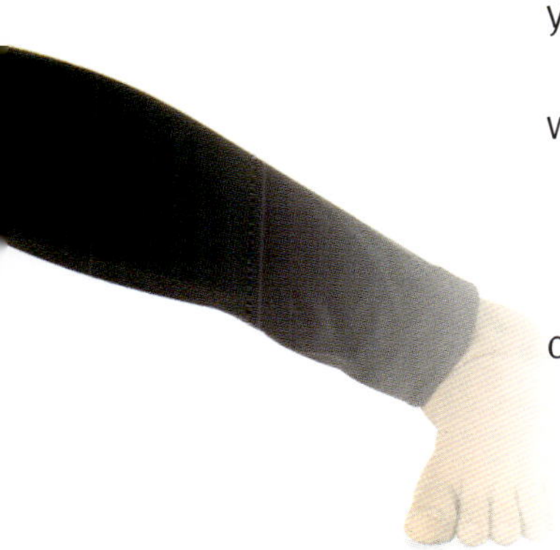

standing tall

Achieving 'perfect posture' is not always a realistic goal. Years of stress and trauma have embedded themselves in the muscles and fascia, and compensatory ways of moving have been developed in response to injuries or pains. This results in protective patterns of holding the body being erected like physiological scaffolding. Don't despair if you have less than ideal alignment: most of us do. For change to occur, your first step has been to become aware of the irregularities. The next step is regular practice with attention both to alignment and undoing muscular tension. Over time, yoga can help to balance the body.

The vertebral column has four curves. When a baby is born its whole spine is a convex 'C' shape. When the infant starts to raise its head the inward (concave) curve of the cervical vertebrae of its neck is formed. On sitting upright, the concave curve in its lower back (lumbar region) develops. The fourth curve is at the base of the spine, where the sacrum and tailbone (coccyx) maintain their original convex shape.

These curves act protectively as a kind of shock absorber. Although we often talk about a 'straight back', we don't actually mean one straight line. Rather, a healthy spine will have a balance between these four curves, with no part too flat or too rounded.

An exaggerated rounding of the thoracic region (upper back) is known as a kyphosis. Lordosis is an increased concavity in the lumbar region. Scoliosis is when the spine curves into a 'C' or 'S' shape and is noticeable from behind, not side on.

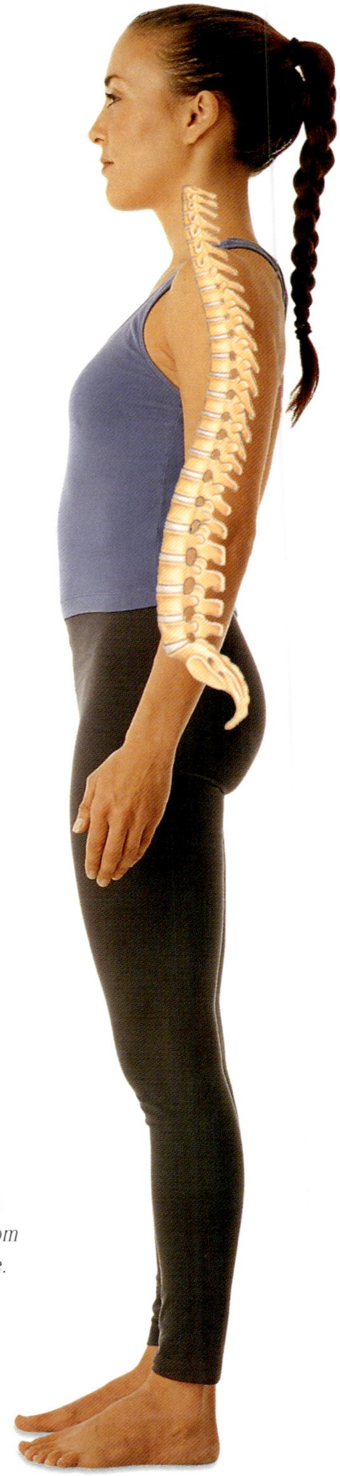

The four curves of the spine, from neck to tailbone.

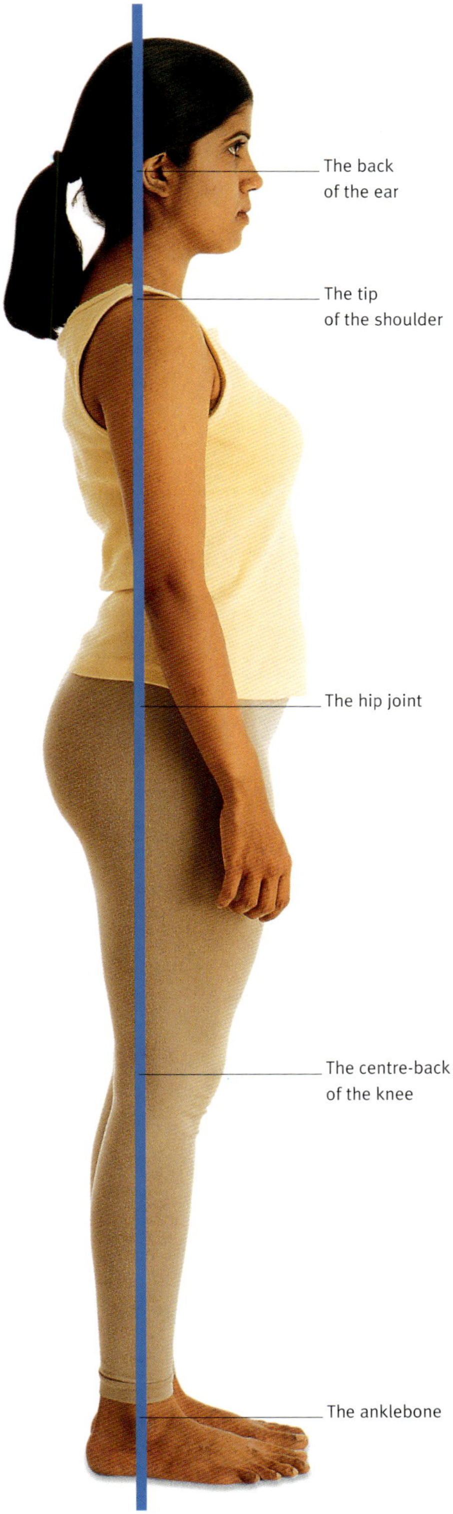

Ask a friend to help assess your posture. Dangle a weighted cord from the side of your head to your ankle so it lines up with the back of your ear. Make a note of which 'landmarks' it passes through on the way to the floor. In an ideal posture, it will pass through the back of your ear, the tip of your shoulder, the centre of your hip joint, the centre-back of your knee and the back edge of your anklebone.

If your plumbline doesn't follow these points, keep in mind that often the disparity doesn't originate from the obvious area, but from lower down. Our base is from the ground up. Irregularities in the feet (such as flattened arches, pigeon-toed or turned out feet) will change the working of the knees. Any problem in the knees (an injury, or hyperextended 'pushed back' knees, for example) will creep up to alter the way the hips work. Any foot, knee or hip problem can potentially affect the back and neck. Commonly, a lower back problem can, over time, spread to become a neck complaint.

tip

At various points throughout the day, stop what you are doing and check your posture. Are you slumped or tense? Take a few moments to adopt a more comfortable, relaxed position.

In an ideal posture, a plumbline would pass through the body points shown here.

samasthiti

equal pose

Use this stable, centred pose to start a short session of standing postures, returning to it at the end of each stretch. You can also practise Samasthiti whenever you are standing during the day.

1 Stand with your feet together or slightly apart, whichever feels more comfortable. Take your awareness to your soles and the distribution of weight between them. Do you have more weight on one foot than the other?
2 If you can balance, close your eyes. Slowly rock your weight from side to side, moving through the centre point of your feet. Now lean forwards and back slowly several times. Finally rest, centred. Bring an element of softness to your feet, so they feel as though they widen outwards.
3 While your feet ground downwards, move your awareness to your legs and get a sense of extending up towards the sky, starting at the ankle joints.
4 Expand your awareness to your torso. Let your pelvis be in a neutral position, tilted neither forward nor back. (For more information, see Exploration: The Role of the Hips in Forward Bends, pages 72–73.)
5 Exhale tension out of the spine so it is released to grow taller. Your abdomen moves in and out in time with your slow, rhythmic breath.
6 If you tend to round your back and 'collapse' in your chest area, lift your breastbone gently towards the chin. Make it subtle, so your floating ribs don't jut out. If you carry your chest expanded to the extent that you bring tension into your lower back, soften it and let go.
7 Drop your shoulders and let them hang relaxed. Aim for a feeling of width between the tips of your shoulders. Let your arms hang, with your fingers naturally slightly.
8 With your shoulders released, you will feel that your neck can extend up. The head is heavy but sometimes part of this weight is psychological. Try to let this unnecessary weight fly off so your head balances in a light, balloon-like way on the top of your neck. Take slow, deep, steady breaths in this pose.

tip

If you find it difficult to balance, take your feet hip-width apart. You can also practise the pose against a wall, which will give you stability and help you to align yourself correctly.

parsvakonasana

side angle stretch

This pose gives a great stretch along the whole side of your body. If your head feels uncomfortable looking up in this pose, or the other standing poses, then look straight ahead.

Soften your shoulders down to release and lengthen the neck.

1 From Samasthiti, take your feet far apart. Turning from the top of your thigh, turn your left leg and foot inwards 15 degrees. Turn your right foot out 90 degrees. Stretch your arms out to the sides. Bend your right knee to 90 degrees. Press into the floor with your back foot to spread your weight evenly between both feet.

2 Bring your right elbow to your thigh. Use your elbow to press your knee back, so it bends in the same direction as your middle toe. This elbow pressure aids the twist in your torso, so the navel and chest begin to turn upwards. Stretch your left arm straight up, reaching your fingers high. If this is where you stay for today, hold this position for five breaths. If you want to go further, take a few breaths here before proceeding.

3 To continue to the final pose, exhale and extend your torso sideways as you bring your right hand to the floor. Reach your left arm overhead and stretch it away from your back foot. Lower your hips and keep your front knee at a right angle. Look straight ahead or just in front of the left upper arm. Build the time in the pose to ten breaths. Repeat on the other side.

tip

If you find your bent knee angles off towards your big toe, and you have trouble keeping it lined up over your middle toe, turn the whole foot out a little.

You might need to widen the distance between your feet in order to straighten the line from your left foot to your left hand.

! DON'T BEND THE FRONT KNEE TO MORE THAN A 90 DEGREE ANGLE. IF YOU FIND YOUR KNEE IN FRONT OF YOUR ANKLE, YOU NEED TO WIDEN YOUR STANCE.

trikonasana

triangle pose

This pose strengthens the legs and ankles, opens the hips and gives the trunk a strong side stretch.

Keep the back hip well back so it stays in-line with the front hip.

1 From Samasthiti (see page 46), jump or step the feet to twice hip-width apart. Turning from the thighs, turn the left foot in 15 degrees and the right foot out 90 degrees. Keep the knees facing the same direction as the toes. Put your hands on your hips to check your hips are the same height. Adjust if necessary.

2 Stretch the arms out to the sides. Exhale and bend from the top of the right thigh; extend your torso and right arm to the right. Feel the right side of your trunk growing longer before putting your right hand on to your thigh or shin. Bring your left arm into the air, following the line of your right arm.

3 Keep the back of your neck long and look straight ahead, or tuck your chin slightly in and turn your head and gaze at your left thumb.

4 The hip bones, perineum, shoulders and hands should be on the same line as your feet. If you find your hips are back and your shoulders are forward of this line, then bring the supporting hand higher up your leg. Hold for five to ten breaths and then repeat on the left side.

tip

In these wide stance standing poses, line up your feet so that the heel of your front foot bisects the centre of your back foot.

Stretch the lifted arm from the armpit, keeping it steady as you reach up.

virabhadrasana I

warrior I

This courageous pose, named after the powerful hero Virabhadra, gathers strength from its solid base for the triumphant lifted chest and raised arms.

tip

To level your hips more easily, turn in your back foot until it's almost parallel with your front foot. For greater ease, lift the back heel off the floor.

1 Stand with your legs about twice shoulder-width apart. Moving from the top of your left thigh, turn in your left leg and foot to 45–60 degrees. Take your right leg and foot out to 90 degrees and bring your upper body to face over your right leg. Your left hip will tend to be further back than your right; soften it forward to bring hips level. Bend your right knee to 90 degrees. (You can broaden your stance, if necessary.) As you bend the front knee, your back knee will tend to follow, but keep it straight by pressing your back heel away.

2 Take your arms out to the sides, turn the palms up and raise the arms overhead to join the palms. Stretch up and raise your shoulders. Look up between the palms and gaze at your thumbs. Lift your breastbone away from your pubic bone and breathe deeply. After ten breaths, inhale as you come up out of the pose. Re-centre in Samasthiti (see page 46) or move to the left side to repeat.

prasarita padottanasana

wide leg stretch

In the flowing, twisting action, use your breath as the starting point. Rather than adjusting your breath to follow your movement, time your movement to follow your breath.

yogic thought

There are two types of yoga poses – conscious and unconscious. Working consciously will consistently deepen your practice.

Deepen concentration by fixing your gaze on your thumb.

1 Stand with the feet wide apart. Exhale and fold forward. Take your left palm to the floor directly under your breastbone, arm straight. On a long, smooth inhalation, sweep your right hand out and up until it is on the same line as your left arm. Follow the moving thumb with your eyes. Time the movement so that your inhalation finishes just when your hand reaches the top. Pause briefly until you are ready to exhale and windmill your hand out and down to reach the floor just as your exhalation tapers out. Now change arms. Inhale your left hand out and up, and exhale it slowly down, keeping the flow of your breath constant. Continue for six more rounds.

You should feel the stretch on your inner thigh.

2 On the final round, hold your top arm in the air. Feel the stretch on your inner thigh. Deepen the twist at your waist and move the top arm even further around and take five full breaths.

3 Come up and rest if necessary and then resume the wide leg stance. Position both palms shoulder width apart on the floor and use them to lever yourself forward. Bend your elbows and walk both hands back between your legs to hold for five to ten breaths. Inhale to come up.

uttanasana

intense forward stretch

As the translation of the Sanskrit implies, this is a strong forward bend. However, it can also be used more passively to rest, offering a lesson in 'undoing' rather than 'doing'.

1 Stand with your feet hip-width apart. Place your hands on your hips and, inhaling, squeeze your elbows closer together behind. Expand your chest so you get a sense of the breastbone moving up and away from the pubic bone. Exhale and, hinging at the hips, fold your torso over your legs. If your hamstrings are tight, bend your knees to access the hinging action of the hips before folding forward.

2 With knees bent or straight, maintain your fullest possible forward fold. As your hands grasp, ease your elbows to the sides. Being upside-down, your shoulders will tend to fall towards the floor. Slide your shoulder blades towards your hips to unhunch them.

3 Grasp your calves or ankles or loop your big toes with your fingers. Straighten your arms, look up and, for the duration of several inhalations, increase the distance between your pubic bone and the base of your throat.

4 If your knees are bent, use each exhalation to work the legs straighter. If your legs are straight, firm the front thigh muscles and bring your hips forward aiming to have the hip joints directly over your ankles. To deepen the pose, lift your seat bones towards the sky and lengthen the back of your waist.

5 You can use the final pose when you need to rest during your yoga session, or as a tension releaser at any time. Bend your knees and fold forward. Your chest will hang closer to your thighs so there is a sense of dangling over from the hips. Take plenty of time to access the feeling of release in the upper body. Spread this rag-doll quality through the body. Relax the back of your neck so it feels long and the crown of the head is closest to the floor. Your arms will hang passively and your fingers curl naturally as your spine begins to lengthen through release. Breathe slowly and steadily. To come up, deepen the knee bend and, over several breaths, roll up through the spine.

tip

Working the feet correctly in the standing poses helps retrain flat feet. Anchor your inner heel and mound of your big toe and, without rolling your ankles out, lift your arches so they are like rainbows.

parsvottanasana

chest to leg extension

This pose will help stretch not only legs and chest but the whole body.

1 From Samasthiti (see page 46), take your feet to twice shoulder width apart. Turn your right knee and foot in 60 degrees. Turn your left thigh, knee and foot out 90 degrees. Open your right groin, so that your upper body can face more over the left leg. Your right hip can then move forwards to align with your left and you can better line up your breastbone with the inside of your left thigh.

2 Take the backs of your hands as high as possible between your shoulder blades. Roll the shoulders and elbows back as you press your palms together into prayer pose. If your shoulders are tight, try holding your elbows behind your back. As a preparation for folding forward, inhale, lift your chest and look up.

tip

To help your balance, mentally anchor down your front big toe and the heel of your back foot.

3 Exhale and extend your torso forward and out before beginning the downward movement over your left thigh. Once you are in the pose, remind your knees to stay straight. Hold the pose for five to ten breaths before repeating on the other side.

4 While you develop your flexibility in this pose, practising using a chair keeps your back straight and your chest open.

garudasana
eagle pose

Grounding and concentration are keys to balance poses such as this.

1 From Samasthiti (see page 46), focus your gaze on a fixed point level with your eyes. Tune into the connection between the soles of your feet and the earth. Focus this awareness on your right foot and bend the left knee. Bend your left leg strongly, and use the momentum to take your right leg around your left. Hook your right toes around the left calf.

keeping your *balance*

Balance poses such as Garudasana can feel very difficult when you first start practising yoga. Most of us have developed distortions and imbalances in our general posture and so it is hard to remain steady in these unfamiliar positions. However, the body is very adaptable and if you persevere over several weeks, balance poses will soon start to become much easier. It will help if you look at a fixed point straight ahead such as a mark on the wall, and if you keep your breathing smooth and steady throughout the pose.

As well as helping your physical coordination and steadiness, balance poses also help to quieten the mind. The mental awareness needed to perform them develops greater concentration and increased calmness. Balance postures also work on the nervous system, and they are often recommended for the relief of stress and anxiety. For the best results, you should practise these postures on a regular basis.

2 Now wrap your arms by crossing your elbows left over right and bringing the palms to face each other. The fingers of your right hand should be high up towards those of your right. You will be able to breathe into the chest more fully if you raise the elbows to shoulder level. If this is easy for you, roll your shoulders back and down. To stretch your shoulders further, ease your forearms forwards so your thumbs move away from your nose. Maintain the pose for ten breaths, before unwrapping, regrounding and repeating on the other side.

tip

Roving eyes will distract you by taking your awareness elsewhere. Keep the eyes steady in all the poses.

5 BackBends

Back bends are extremely invigorating, and help to develop willpower, determination and courage. They are all-involving: in a strong back bend, it is hard to think about anything else. This makes them good postures for freeing yourself from distracting thoughts. They also expand and lift the heart centre at the chest, creating space for joy to reside in the body.

Bending backwards takes you into unfamiliar territory. While we often bend forwards in our day to day lives, we rarely bend backwards. These asanas encourage us to conquer the fear of the unknown and build faith in ourselves.

Take care when performing back bends in short, ten-minute sessions. You should always warm up with standing postures before beginning back bends, and follow them with some twists and forward bends to release your back and cool the system. People with hypertension or back problems should work with a teacher. Back bends should be avoided during menstruation.

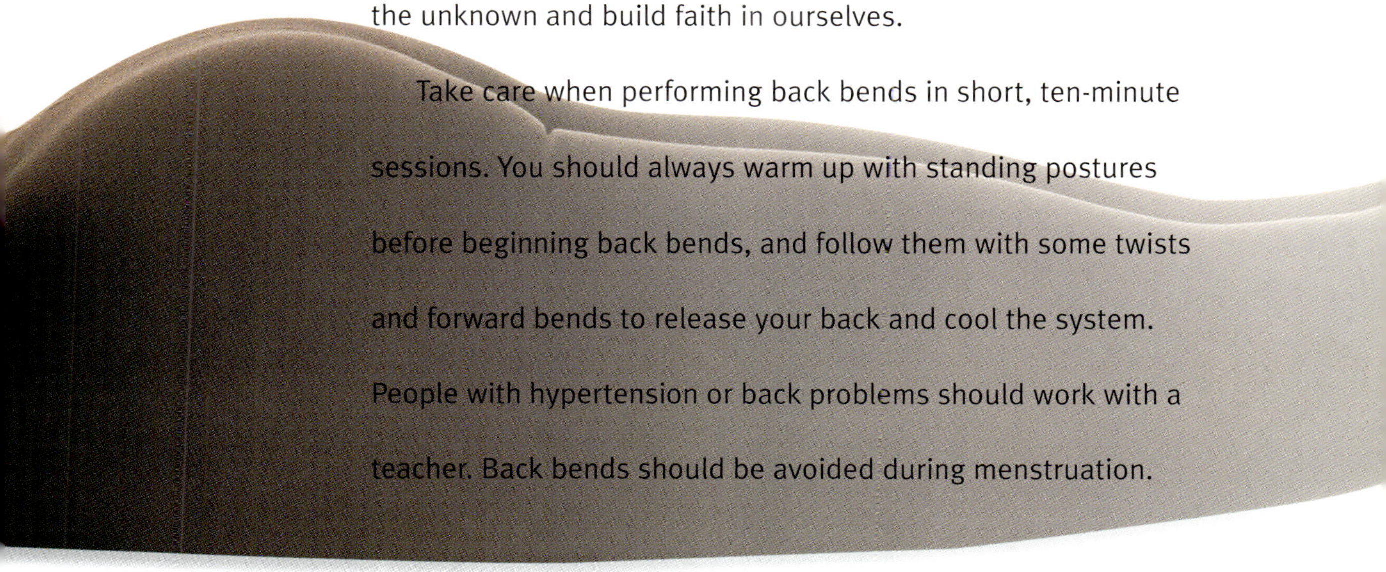

exploration

preparations for back bending

Rehearse the isolated movements for bending backwards before you unite them in the back bending asanas.

1 Sit on your heels and interlace your fingers behind your head, keeping your shoulders relaxed. As you inhale open your elbows out to the side and back. Keeping your head well supported, look up. Keep the back of your neck long: this feeling is what you are aiming for in back bends such as the cobra (see pages 62–63) and locust poses (see pages 64–65).

2 Exhale and slowly bring your elbows closer together in front of you, as you take your chin towards your breastbone. Don't press the head down with your hands. Move between these two positions ten times. With each inhalation, focus on the curving of your upper back and neck. Feel the expansion in your ribs. Let each exhalation be long and slow as you soften your upper body.

You will experience a feeling of the back being 'lengthened'.

3 Now come up to a kneeling position. Interlace your fingers behind you, so your knuckles rest on either side of the spine below the shoulder blades. Take time to anchor down through the knees. Lengthen your front thighs by tucking your tailbone under and opening your groin. On an inhalation, press your hands into your back, squeeze your elbows towards each other and lift your breastbone as you bend backwards. Maintain the long neck from the first exercise and don't take your neck back beyond its comfort level.

If the pelvis were a bowl full of water, this tilting motion would tip the water out.

4 Press your knuckles into the sides of your spine and, as your chest lifts and opens, get a feeling of lifting the vertebrae up and over them. While you will naturally feel long in the front, maintain the length in the back of your body as much as possible. Remember this feeling of the long back so you can reproduce it in each back bending asana.

5 As you exhale relax your shoulders down and your elbows forwards and come back to a neutral position. Complete ten more rounds.

6 Kneel on your right knee and bend your left leg in front. Place your hands on your hipbones with your thumbs facing back and your fingers forwards.

7 Imagine your pelvis is a container full of water and you want to pour the water out slowly. First, tilt your pelvis forwards so that you feel your fingers move down and your thumbs move up as if you were pouring the water out of the front.

8 Now tip your pelvis back the other way, as if you were pouring water behind you. Your fingers raise up and the curve in your lower back flattens out. Do it slowly and you will feel a deep stretch in the front of the left thigh.

9 This tipping back action is good practice for safe back bending. Back bends start from the very base of the spine, not the lumbar region. The tailbone needs to lengthen down towards the ground. This initial flattening out of the lower back lengthens the vertebrae away from each other, as preparation for a long, deep curve.

10 Keep your chest and shoulders steady as you inhale while tipping forwards and exhale while tipping backwards. Allow plenty of time to begin to isolate this movement.

bhujangasana

cobra pose

As you form the shape of a cobra, it's like rising up to meet an obstacle in your path. Like all back bends, this pose helps to foster determination and willpower.

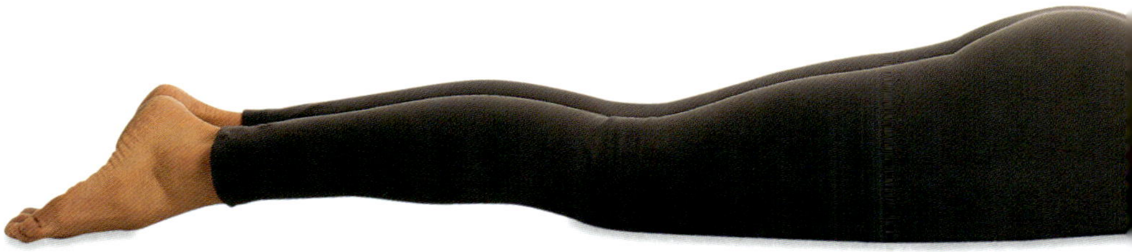

1 Lie on your front with your feet together and your forehead touching the floor. Place your palms on the floor so your fingertips are level with the tips of the shoulders, and your elbows are in the air. Roll your shoulders back and down away from your ears, so they move towards your hips. Squeeze your elbows towards each other and feel the length in the back of the neck.

2 Slightly tilt your pelvis by pressing your pubic bone to the floor. When you do this, you can reach your toes back further and the back of your waist lengthens.

3 Curl your head and shoulders up as far as you can without taking weight on your hands. Hold this position to find out which back muscles need to work. Now press the hands to the floor as you curve up higher, shoulders down and neck long. Your elbows stay deeply bent and your hips stay on the floor. Hold three repetitions for ten breaths. When you inhale deeply, your abdominal organs are massaged as your abdomen presses on the floor.

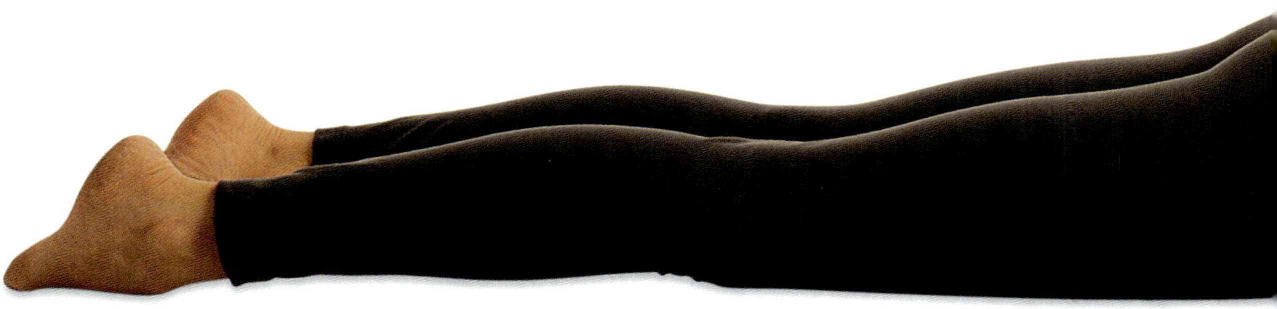

tip

From your starting position, lift one leg at a time and stretch it back. Observe how this gives more length in the lower back.

4 Extend the inner body as you 'pump' the breastbone forward and up on each inhalation. Lower the shoulders and the outer body on each exhalation to lengthen the inner body.

5 Make a pillow with your hands and rest with your head to alternate sides between each repetition.

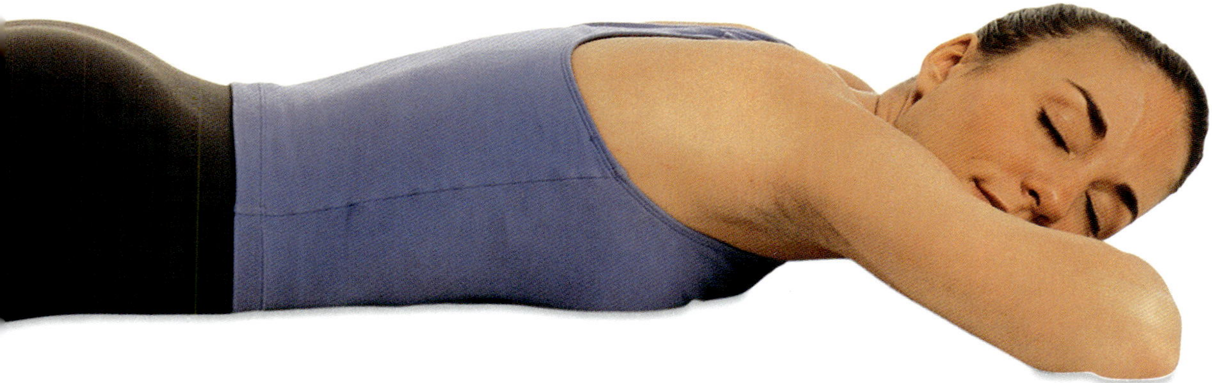

salabhasana

locust pose

This pose is strengthening for the back and opening for the chest. Its action on the back works best if you keep your ankles together.

1 Lie on your front with your feet together and your forehead on the floor, arms by your side. Tuck your toes under, stretch your heels away and lift up the knees. Firm your thighs and keep both legs straight. Move your tailbone towards your feet and stretch both heels back to elongate the back.

2 Now flick your toes away and lift your straight legs up in the air. Lift your arms and curl your head and chest up off the floor. Lengthen the crown of your head and your tailbone away from each other. Your back bend will deepen as you press both shoulders away from your ears and reach your fingers toward the toes. Build to hold three repetitions for ten breaths each. Between repetitions, relax down, turn your head to one side and observe your breathing as it returns to normal.

> If you suffer from back problems, keep your chest on the floor and lift one leg at a time, stretching it well back. Then keep your feet well anchored to the floor and lift only your upper body and arms.

step into the *unknown*

While we intimately know the fronts of our bodies, the best view we are likely to have had of our backs is second-hand, through a mirror. Back bends are a way of gaining access to this important area of the body, allowing you to fully explore it.

Practising back bends can give rise to feelings of fear or other deep emotions. This is because the poses encourage us to take a step into the unknown. At the same time, they expand and open the chest and heart area, encouraging us to embrace life. This can be exhilarating and energizing, but it can also feel very challenging.

If you find back bends difficult, take them slowly. Work gently, keeping your breathing deep and steady. Find your edge and breathe as you allow yourself to relax into it. Working with an experienced teacher will help you to get the most from your back bends.

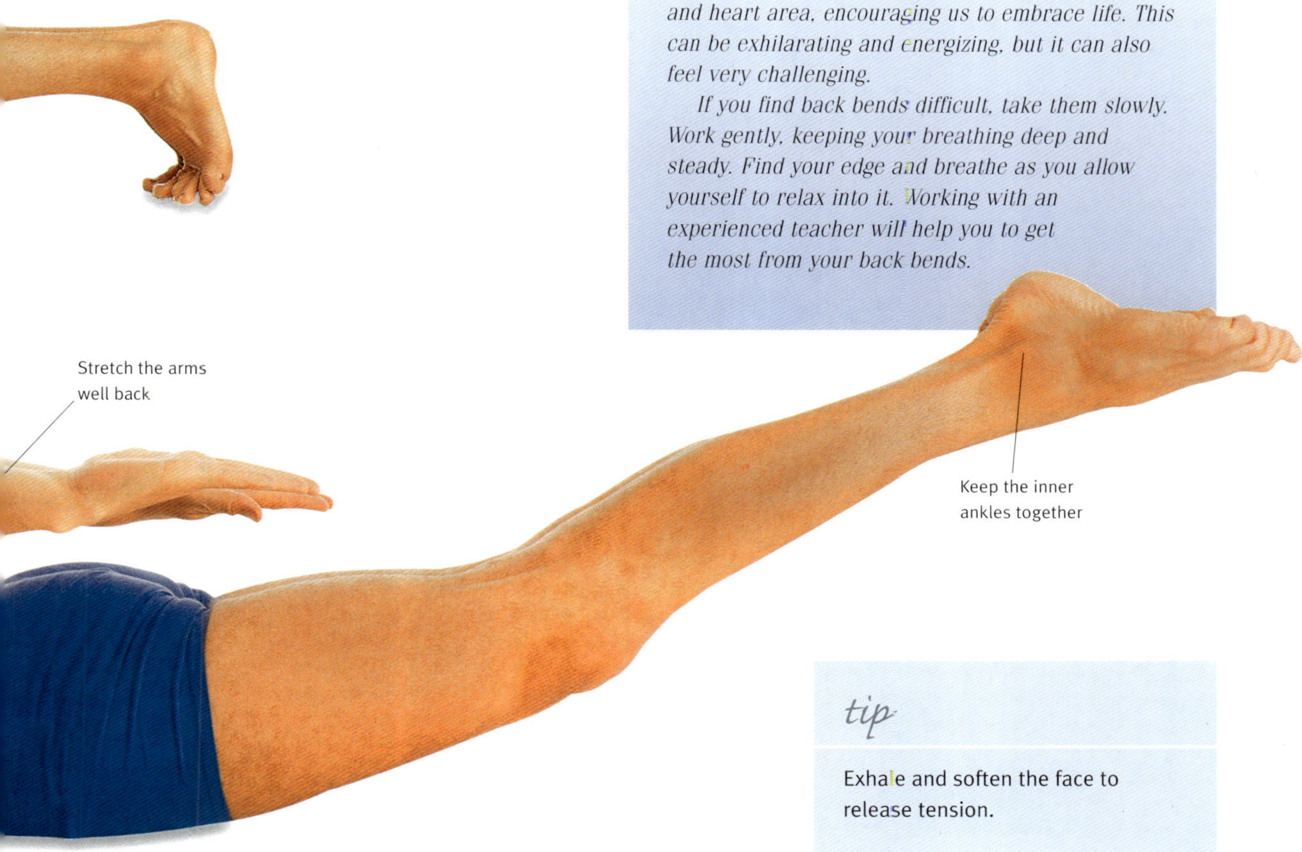

tip

Exhale and soften the face to release tension.

setu bandhasana

bridge pose

tip

Don't let your knees splay apart – keep them only as wide as your hips.

As you open your chest, expand your heart centre in this pose.

1 Lie on your back with the knees bent up. Place your feet 15cm (6in) away from your buttocks and have them as wide as your hipbones.

2 Begin by tilting your pelvis slightly so your buttocks move off the ground. Your lower, middle and upper back will still be connected to the floor. Take several breaths in this position.

3 Now, while constantly stretching your knees away, slowly lift your hips higher. With your hips raised up, tuck your shoulders under one by one. Squeeze the shoulder blades in together and shift more weight onto the tips of the shoulders. If your elbows can straighten, interlace your fingers and press them down to lift and open the chest.

4 A bridge reaches in both directions to the river banks. While the breastbone moves toward your chin, the tailbone moves toward the knees. After holding for five to ten breaths come down and rest. Repeat twice.

yogic thought

Have patience as you approach each new edge in a pose. Respect the body and wait for it to let you in.

matsyasana

fish pose

Matsyasana hyperextends the neck. It is excellent after both the Sarvangasana (pages 98–99) and Halasana (page 102) where the neck is strongly flexed.

tip

Bring your awareness to the back of the body. Develop the sensitivity of the skin on the back as it thins out in each back bend.

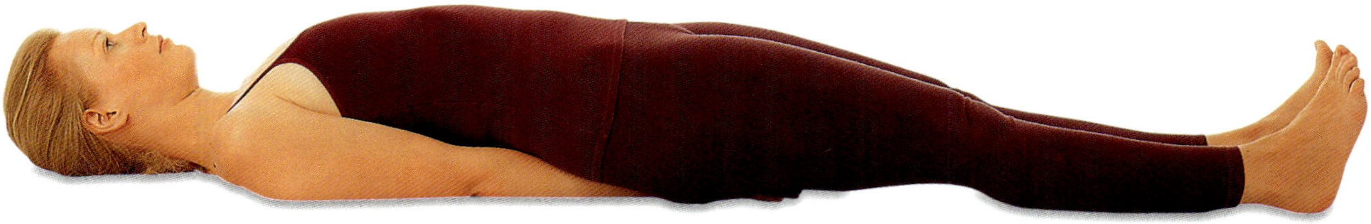

1 Lying on your back, take your hands, palms down, under your thighs. Reach your fingertips as far as you can towards the backs of the knees.

2 Inhale and come up so you are resting on your elbows. Squeeze your shoulder blades in together, then exhale and release the crown of your head lightly to the floor. Expand your chest and draw each inhalation deeper. In Matsyasana, only about 10 per cent of your weight is on the crown of the head, and the rest is supported by the elbows and lower body. Hold for five to ten breaths.

3 To come up, inhale strongly as you move the weight forward onto your elbows and lift your head. Bring your chin to your chest as you lower down to rest on your back. Release your neck by gently turning your head to take alternate ears to the floor.

chakrasana

wheel pose

Recharge with this demanding, but highly energizing pose.

1 Lie on your back, with your knees bent and your feet 20cm (8in) from your buttocks. Place your hands near the shoulders, fingers pointing in the direction of the hips. Take some time to breathe while anchoring down through your heels.

2 Lift your hips up, then inhale and lift up on to the crown of your head. Breathe here as you mentally prepare to lift all the way up. Pressurize the palms, inhale and straighten the arms to lift into the full position.

> ! THIS POSE IS NOT ADVISABLE IN CASES OF SLIPPED DISC, HERNIA, HEART PROBLEMS OR HIGH BLOOD PRESSURE, OR DURING MENSTRUATION, PREGNANCY OR THE POST-NATAL PERIOD.

tip

Going into and coming out of a pose is part of your whole practice of yoga. Never collapse out of a pose. Come out with awareness.

3 Now you are up, make a few adjustments. In the effort of coming up, your toes will tend to turn out and your knees move apart. Bring your feet back to parallel, then reposition your knees over your feet.

4 While in the classic pose the heels are on the ground, come onto your tiptoes until you can straighten the arms. Keep the heels up if you need to build the flexibility to prevent compressing your lower back when the heels are lowered. Now visualize a circle of energy moving between the hands and the toes. Lift and move your sacrum around this wheel towards your knees. Push up into the fronts of your thighs and open your groin more. Expand the chest.

5 Hold and breathe for five to ten breaths. When you come down, tuck the chin in and lower down with control. Rest and feel the difference in your body and mind after doing this pose. Repeat twice more – it usually feels best of all the third time.

6 Ease out your back by hugging your knees into your chest and rocking slowly from side to side. The slower you rock, the nicer this massage feels.

6 Forward Bends and Seated Poses

After bending backwards, you need to bend forwards to stretch the whole back of the body and increase the vitality of the spine. Forward bends nourish the abdominal organs, so they aid digestion and enhance general well-being.

The act of bending forwards promotes introspection and helps quieten the mind. Folding into yourself lets you access your intuitive self and become more self-aware.

You can spend ten minutes just doing forward bends when you are tired or after a hard day. Increase the restorative effect by using props; stack up pillows or bolsters and drop your forehead onto them as you fold over. This allows the frontal lobe of the brain to rest, which has a calming effect.

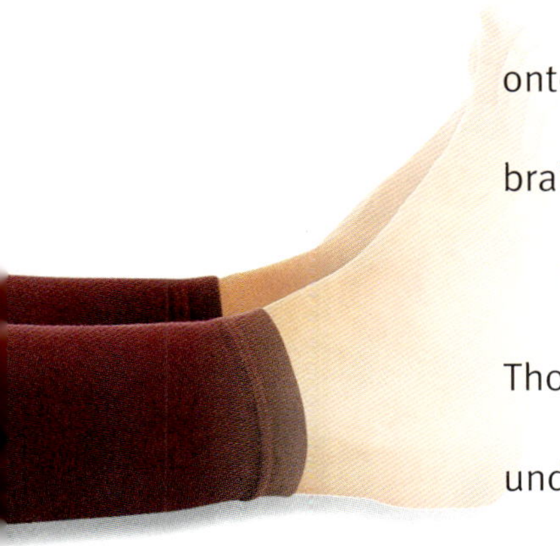

People with severe depression should avoid forward bends. Those suffering from a slipped disc need to modify the bends under the guidance of an experienced teacher.

exploration

the role of the hips in forward bends

Isolate the hip movement for correct alignment in forward bends.

1 Sit on a chair and place your hands on your hipbones, fingers facing forwards. Rock the pelvis back so your thumbs move down and fingers tilt up. Your lower back will feel as though it flattens out on this upward tilting.

2 The key movement for forward bends is as follows. Tilt your pelvis forwards so your fingers move forward and down. The desired action comes from the hip joint. Your thighbones stay still and you are rotating the hip socket around the stationary head of the thighbone. Tilt the hips slowly back and forth. It may take a while for the movement to come. It is vital in forward bending to move the stretch to the back of the thighs and not overstretch the lower back.

3 A common mistake if this hip action comes with difficulty is to sway the chest back and forth, causing the floating ribs to jut out. In the correct action, the vertebral column stays quite straight; the chest and shoulders move only slightly.

4 Once you have this feeling, refine this movement. Raise your seat 20cm (8in) from the floor by sitting on a small stool or firm cushions. Tilt back and forth, repeating the action of rotating your pelvis around the heads of the thigh bones. As you tilt forward, the crease at the top of your thighs will deepen and you may feel your seat bones jut out more behind you.

Incorrect
A common mistake is to round the back as you bend. Always keep your back as flat as possible, and bend from the hips as you extend forwards.

5 For the third stage, sit on the floor and practise this same movement. If, from this lower position, you can't access it, bend your knees. It helps if you can feel your seat bones on the floor, so use your hands to move your buttock flesh back and out to the sides.

6 If it feels very difficult, as if your hips are frozen, it could be a sign of tight hamstrings. If your pelvis tilts backwards when you sit up straight, and your stomach muscles have to work strongly just to keep you upright, then modify your starting position. Lift your seat with a cushion, and bend your knees if necessary.

7 A common error when stretching fully forward is to round the back and hunch the shoulders in an effort to push the head down as far as possible. Forward bends originate at the hips, which work almost like a simple hinge joint.

8 As you hinge forwards, keep your back straight so that your navel will reach your thighs before your chest reaches your knees. Only then will your nose come to your shins. Remind yourself of this during every forward bend, and think of forward folding rather than bending.

adho mukha svanasana

downward-facing dog

This is an excellent pose for stretching and strengthening the whole body. Though it may not feel like it at first, with practice it can become very restful.

1 Begin on all fours. Have your knees and feet hip width apart. Walk your hands forwards 15cm (6in) so they are in front of, not directly below, your shoulders. To protect your wrists, check that your middle fingers are facing straight forwards. Get a sense of your hands pressing into the earth. Feel how your weight is distributed on the palms. Aim for an even spread from the base of your hand right to your fingertips.

2 Tuck your toes under and lift your hips high until you are in an inverted V position. Bend your right knee and exhale as you stretch your left heel towards the floor. Change sides and allow the muscles on the back of your right leg to release. Working with the breath, warm your hamstrings by moving back and forth from right to left.

tip

Use downward-facing dog as a link between other postures in your yoga practice.

3 To come into the final position, inhale and rise on to the tips of your toes so your hips lift high. Keep your hips as high in the air as you can while you exhale and stretch the heels down to the floor so that your legs seem to grow longer.

deepen it

Play with this pose by practising the backwards and forwards pelvic tilt (see page 72). It gives you the option of increasing flexibility in the backs of the thighs or stretching more into the lower back to release tension there instead.

4 Widen the shoulder blades apart by rolling your upper arms outwards. Aim for one straight line from wrists to buttocks. Root the mounds of your thumbs and index fingers to keep the pressure evenly spread through your palms. In this inverted position, the spine hangs down from the hips. Get a sense of extension in your spine through letting go, rather than using effort, to lengthen. Maintain the downward-facing dog pose for five to 15 steady breaths.

5 To rest after this pose, bring your big toes together, knees wide apart, and rest your hips back to your heels until the breath has steadied.

trianga mukhaikapada paschimottanasana

three-limbed bend

> *tip*
>
> Keep the ankle of the straight leg flexed and stretch the heel away in all the forward bends.

Though it can feel awkward at first, due to its particular action on the hips, this pose is a good lead off for the seated forward bends.

1 Sit on the floor with your legs outstretched. Bend your right leg back to bring your heel near to your hip. Adjust your position by leaning to the left and with your right hand, roll your calf flesh out to the right, and 'iron' it down towards the heel. You will tend to tilt to the left, so mentally anchor your right seatbone down.

2 Before you think about going forward, it's useful to sit erect and breathe yourself taller for a short while. When you are ready, inhale as you bring your arms overhead, and exhale as you extend forward to grasp your calf, ankle or foot. Inhale, lift your chest and look up. Exhale, bend your elbows to the sides, and fold forward with a flat back and open chest. Hold for five to ten breaths before repeating on the other side.

3 To lessen tilting and to keep your spine straight, have a folded blanket under your bent leg side.

janu sirsasana

head beyond the knee pose

Make a big job less daunting by dividing it in half. Use this pose to prepare for Paschimottanasana (see pages 78–79) by stretching one leg at a time.

1 Sit with both legs straight in front of you. Bend your right leg out to the side so your heel is near your groin, and 3cm (1in) away from your left inner thigh. Don't let your toes slip under your thigh. Stretch your left heel away so that your knee and toes point straight up.

2 You will find this pose easier with a preparatory twist. Taking your left hand behind you and your right hand to the outer left knee, twist left for a few breaths.

deepen it

Try a more advanced way of working to still the fluctuations in the body. If you hold a pose for ten breaths, use the first three to adjust and deepen it. For the remaining seven, hold still and open yourself to perceive and observe. You are moving neither away from nor towards anything. Find the still point.

3 Untwist slightly, and line up your breastbone so that it is over your left thigh. Inhale and lengthen up from your pubic bone to the base of your throat. Exhale and fold forwards. Hold your calf, side of the foot or left wrist around the foot. Use your arms to lever your torso deeper over your left thigh.

4 Sitting on a folded blanket allows you to fold a little deeper. Loop a belt around your foot to maintain correct alignment in the forward bends.

paschimottanasana

stretch on the body's west side

Traditionally the west side of the body relates to the back of the body and the outer self. In this sequence, use visualization as you fold into the east side – your inner self.

Exhale and sweep your hands down the front of your body.

1 Sit quietly and think of some way you would like to spring-clean your life. Perhaps you feel your life could be better with less aggression, hate or envy. Maybe you would like to remove a health problem, or feelings of doubt, indecision or laziness. Keeping in mind the quality you decide on, inhale to bring your hands near your chest.

2 Now exhale and sweep your hands down the entire front of your body and out past your feet. Inhale as you bring your arms up in a wide arc and exhale as you push away what is unwanted, out of your body and out of your life. Repeat six more of these cleansing cycles, or as many as you feel necessary.

Visualization is an important step to creating a life as you want it.

tip

Yoga is not impulsive. Perform asanas slowly to become aware of your actions, reactions, intentions and thoughts. Leave time to receive feedback from your body between poses.

3 Now pause and consider what you would like more of in your life. Would you feel better off with more compassion, enthusiasm, love, joy or humility in your life? Do you seek contentment, truth or wisdom?

4 This time reverse the flow. Start with your hands at your feet and draw your palms up close to your body as you sweep that desired quality into your life. Lean back, take your arms up in the air, exhale and reach forward. Inhale and sweep up again to continue welcoming that special quality. Repeat six more cycles, or more if you like.

5 Now prepare to hold the pose steady. Grasp your feet, ankles or calves. Inhale and lift the chest up so the front of the torso is long. Exhale to extend forward. In this folded position, your back is turned on what is unwelcome and you can gather that special quality into your world. Take long, slow breaths for ten to 15 rounds.

Not concaving your chest will allow your heart centre to open

purvottanasana
stretch on the body's east side

This is a counterpose for Paschimottanasana (see pages 78–79) and other forward bends.

yogic thought

Ahimsa, *or non-violence, is the first point of the first limb of yogic philosophy. Refrain from aggressive behaviour, even verbally, towards others. Ahimsa also includes non-violence to yourself. Be respectful of your body and don't push beyond your limit. An injury is a lack of ahimsa.*

1 Sit on the floor with your legs in front of you. Place the hands on the floor 15cm (6in) behind your hips, fingers pointing forwards. Point your toes away and lift your hips high. As you press your palms into the floor, fully expand your chest and release your neck and head back. Keep your front thigh muscles working and your toes pressing to the floor. Do three repetitions for five to ten breaths each.

2 An easier variation is to begin with bent knees, then lift the hips and chest.

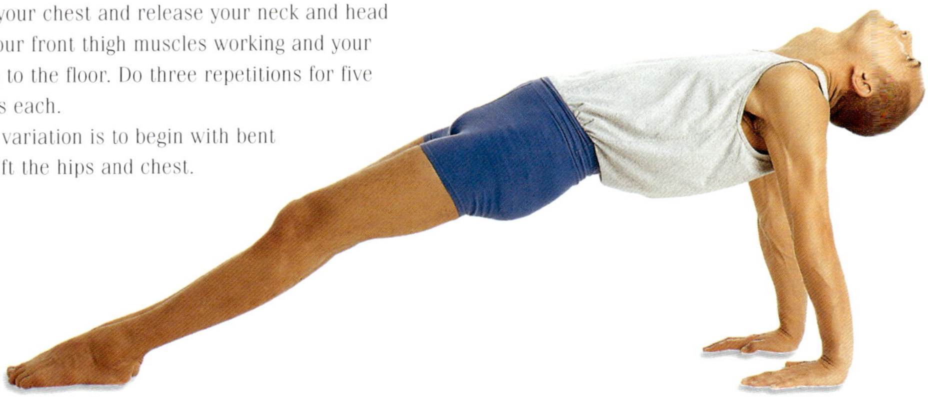

baddha konasana

cobbler's pose

Cobbler's Pose promotes good health in the urinary and reproductive systems. It is helpful during pregnancy or for menstrual disorders. This is a good asana to practise daily, for ten minutes a time.

tip

Don't bounce to release by butterflying your knees up and down. Learn to use the exhalation to soften the tight areas.

1 Sit on the floor and bring the soles of your feet together with the heels near the perineum. Use the pressure of your hands to the floor behind you to tilt the pelvis forward, opening the inner thighs, groin and hips.
2 Although you want your knees as close to the floor as possible, don't force them down. They will release down more easily if you direct them out and back away from the root of the inner thigh.
3 If you can comfortably sit erect without the support of your hands behind you, hold your feet. If not, pressurize your hands on the floor, or sit on folded blankets. With your chest broad and open, breathe into the pose.

4 If your pelvis tips forward easily, bend your elbows into the calves to ease the knees back and down closer to the floor and fold forward. Breathe evenly for five to ten rounds.

yogic thought
The quality of your posture is not measured by how flexible you are. Measure your pose by how steady your breath is.

upavista konasana sequence

seated wide angle pose

As the connective tissue and muscle groups are large, it takes time for them to relax progressively into these forward stretches. In a single sitting, given time and patience you can stretch deeper than you imagined possible.

1 Sit with your legs out to the sides at a 90 degree angle. Check that your kneecaps and toes are not rolling forwards or backwards, but point straight up to the sky. Twist to the right and take your left hand to your outer right knee. Cup your right hand on the floor behind you. This twist/pose prepares you for the wide-legged side stretch. Take five slow breaths. Feel your spine grow taller with each inhalation. On every exhalation feel your waist narrowing as you twist deeper.

2 Untwist slightly so your breastbone is in line with your right thigh. Exhale and stretch forward to reach your right calf or foot. To work deeper into the pose, anchor your left seatbone down to the floor. Turn the toes back and extend through both heels. Hold this position for five to ten full breaths.

tip

In straight leg forward bends, keep your kneecaps and toes pointing directly up. You can even mark a dot at the centre of your knee to remind yourself!

3 Now you are ready for Upavista konasana. Sit up and press your fingertips to the floor behind you so your chest lifts and you tilt your pelvis forward. Just this movement alone will start to stretch the inner thigh and, if you have stiff hips, this may be as far as you go in this pose for today.

4 Inhale and create the sensation of the torso lifting out of the pelvis. Exhale and fold part way forward to grasp both of your calves, ankles or feet. Once more, inhale, lift up a little, lengthen from pubic bone to throat, then exhale out and down. Build to hold this for 20 breaths.

5 Support under your knees with your hands as you bring your legs together.

> ! EASE OFF IF YOU EXPERIENCE TOO MUCH INTENSITY ON THE INNER THIGHS OR PAIN IN THE INNER KNEE.

gomukhasana

cow-face pose

This pose is invaluable for relieving tight hips and shoulders. The arm position is a good stretch to do in ten minutes during a busy day.

1 Sit on the floor with your legs in front of you, knees bent. Reach your left hand under your thigh to grasp your right ankle and pull it around to rest by your left hip. Now take your left foot over the top to rest by your right hip. In the complete pose, your left knee will stack up on top of the right.

2 Take your right arm straight up. Rotating from your shoulder, turn your little finger side to the front. Stretch up from your right hip to your fingertips, bend your elbow and lower your forearm behind you. Grasp your elbow with your left hand and take several breaths as you ease your right hand further down your back. Now release your left arm down. Rotate from the shoulder so your left thumb turns back. Bend the left arm behind you to grasp your hands together. Open your chest as you sit up tall for ten to 15 breaths. Check that your head is straight, not tilting down or off to one side.

This alternative position (described in step 4) offers an easier option.

tip

If you find your top knee stays high in the air, use folded blankets to raise your seat.

3 If you have tight shoulders, walk your hands together using a soft belt.

4 As an alternative, place your left ankle on your right knee. This helps to loosen tight hips.

5 Repeat the exercise on the other side.

navasana

boat pose

Strengthening the abdomen often helps back conditions, too. Develop your strength in ten-minute sessions until you can hold Navasana for three rounds.

1 From a sitting position, lean back on your hands and lift your legs up straight. As you lift your chest, take the small of the back in towards the navel and up. Don't round your back or let your chest sink. Reach your hands forward. Gaze up at your big toes as you hold for five steady breaths.

2 An easier version is to hug your knees into your chest. Feel your abdominal muscles growing stronger as you lift up your chest.

tip

Build up to the full pose with your toes resting lightly on the wall.

yogic thought

Each asana should be steady and comfortable. A measure of your mastery of an asana is whether you can keep your breath steady and comfortable throughout.

bhujapidasana

arm pressure balance

You probably don't require more arm strength than you already have to do this balance. Instead, concentrate on your mental focus in order to balance yourself.

1 Stand with the feet hip-width apart, and bend forward. Take your right arm between and back through your legs. Place the hand on the floor by the outside of your right foot. Bend your knee and take as much of your upper arm behind it as you can so the back of your thigh touches high up on your upper arm. Place the palm flat on the floor, fingers facing forward. To do the same on the left side, you will have to squat to flatten both palms on the floor.

2 Lean forward, bend your elbows to 90 degrees and walk your feet forward towards each other. Lift up through the abdominal region as you raise your head to gaze forwards, and lift your feet up in the air to cross the ankles. Extend the arms and hold for five breaths. Rest down and repeat with your feet crossed the opposite way.

7 Twists

Twisting the trunk gives a gentle squeeze to the internal organs, flushing out deoxygenated blood and allowing fresh blood to enter and nourish the tissues. It's like squeezing soapy water out of a dish sponge, and then immersing it to soak up fresh water.

The twisting pressure has a good massaging effect, too. The kidneys, liver, spleen and digestive system all benefit. Tension in the back can also often be relieved by ten-minute twist sessions.

Apart from being uplifting physically, twisting the torso gives you a mental lift, enhancing vitality and boosting energy. Twisting limbers the vertebral column, which, apart from housing important nerves, nudges the subtle energies of the body upwards to higher centres.

Those with heavy or painful periods should proceed very gently with the twists and focus more on forward bends. Avoid twists in cases of diarrhoea and severe colitis.

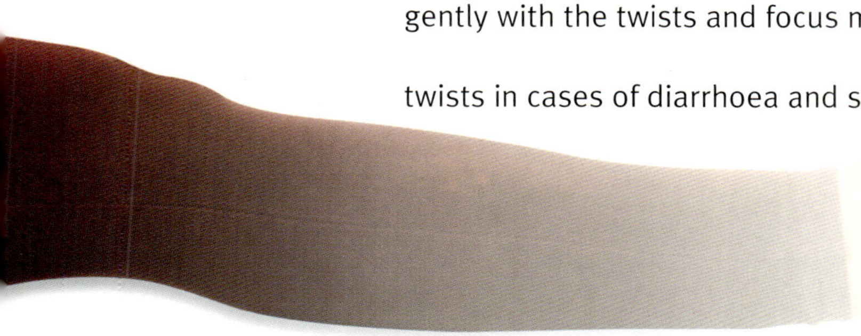

pavritta sukhasana

cross-legged twist

Use this simple cross-legged pose to learn how to twist from bottom to top, and from inside to outside, with awareness. It can be easily practised in ten minutes.

1 Sit cross-legged and slide your feet crossways so the ankles align themselves under the knees. Bring the heels forward so your shinbones are more or less parallel with each other. Bring the fingertips of the right hand to cup the left knee, and those of the left to the floor behind you.

2 The correct twisting action begins at the root of the back. Learn to work in segments to move the twist progressively up your spine so you can apply the same principles to other twists.

3 Pressurize your fingertips down to the floor and inhale taller. To begin the twist, visualize your abdominal organs twisting to the left and, on an exhale, activate the lower abdominal muscles so they move from right to left. On the next exhalation, shunt the middle abdominal muscles left. Visualize an upward spiral of energy. Each time you inhale, feel a lengthening upward of the spine, and on each exhalation, from the core of the body, twist deeper.

4 When you come to involve the chest in the twist, it works better to twist more on the inhale, rather than the exhale. Remembering to use at least one breath per section, turn the ribs more to the left, then bring the shoulders into the twist. Finally, turn your head left to find the position which feels right for your neck. Hold for five to ten breaths, maintaining the feeling of spinning upwards.

5 Unwind and take a moment to feel the effects that the twist has had on your body: sweep over your abdomen, ribs, back, shoulders and the rest of the body. Check in with your mind too. Twist to the other side, then change the way the legs are crossed and repeat.

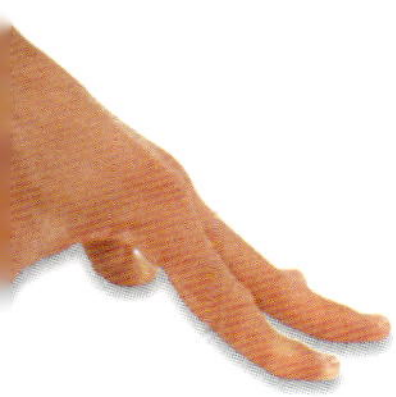

Incorrect

Don't jam the floating ribs forward as you bend the spine backwards. Keep your back straight so your head and neck are over your pelvis. Both shoulders should be roughly the same height from the floor, as should both ears.

marichyasana

sage twist

As you breathe deeply in this pose, the pressure of your thigh against your abdomen will gently massage your abdominal organs.

1 Sit with your legs in front of you. Bend your left knee up and bring your heel close to your buttock. To begin the twist, press into the floor with your left hand, lean back and reach your right hand up to the sky. Take a few breaths to lengthen the right side of the torso.

2 Now exhale, lean forwards and wedge your right elbow by your outer left knee. If possible, slide your right arm away so it contacts your left knee closer to your armpit. Use the instructions in the previous pose, Pavritta Sukhasana (see pages 90–91), to twist upwards in stages. Hold for five to ten breaths, then untwist, re-centre and repeat on the other side.

3 For the full posture, reach your right arm forward beyond the left knee. Rotate from your shoulder to turn your right arm thumb down and wrap it all the way around your knee to clasp your hands together. Grasp a soft belt if necessary, and repeat on the other side.

tip

As twists tend to compress one lung slightly, be aware of the other lung being exercised fully as it fills with air.

jathara parivartanasana

stomach strengthening twist

If you practise regularly, weak abdominal muscles will grow noticeably stronger in a short time.

1 Lie on your back with your arms out to the sides, hands at shoulder level. Bring both legs up in the air. Lift the hips and 'bunny hop' the buttocks to the left.

2 Stretch out through your heels as you hold the left leg steady and exhale your right leg out to the side, toes aiming to fingertips. On your next exhalation, slowly lower your left leg to join the right. Inhale your left leg back to vertical. Inhale and follow with your right leg. Complete five repetitions on each side.

tip

Recovery time will be quicker between poses if you bring your awareness from the front side to the back side of your body.

3 For the full pose, exhale to lower both straight legs to the right. If you can, catch hold of your feet. Stretch both heels away, especially the top one, as you twist your abdominal muscles to the left. Anchor as much of the left side of your trunk to the floor as you can. Turn your head to gaze at your left hand. Hold for five breaths before inhaling both legs up. Do five repetitions on each side. Bend the knees to reduce the difficulty.

8 Inversions

An upside-down position is an opportunity to consider life from a different point of view. When you feel stuck or in need of inspiration, an inverted posture can help to alter your mindset.

When you are inverted, blood flows more easily to the upper body. Cerebral function is aided due to this extra nourishment, so inversions help combat lethargy. Inversions are a form of aerobic exercise, too. Blood flows more easily to the heart, which then fills more quickly and increases its activity to pump the blood back out. This increased circulation can provide an impromptu boost in a ten-minute session.

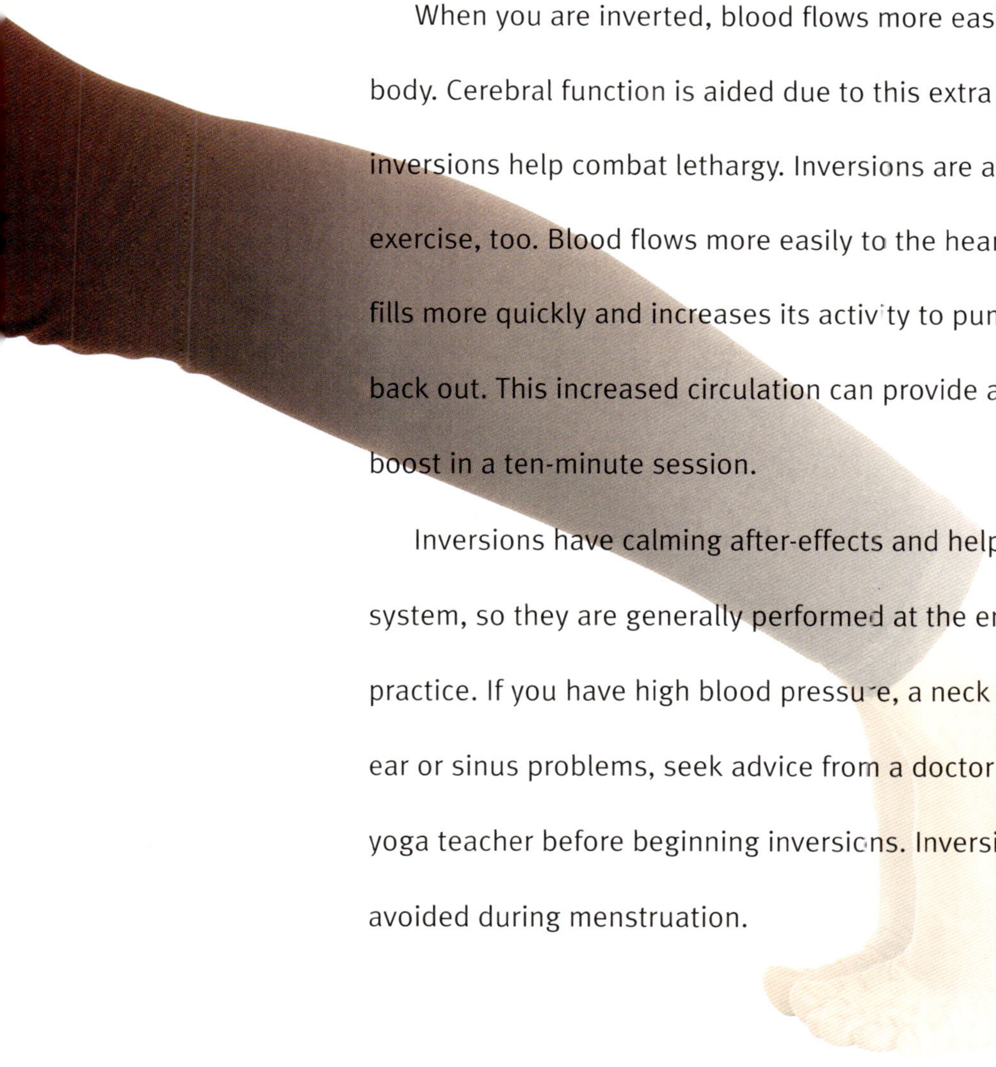

Inversions have calming after-effects and help to cool the system, so they are generally performed at the end of asana practice. If you have high blood pressure, a neck problem, eye, ear or sinus problems, seek advice from a doctor or experienced yoga teacher before beginning inversions. Inversions should be avoided during menstruation.

sarvangasana

shoulderstand

The shoulderstand stimulates circulation to the thyroid and parathyroid glands, and regulates blood flow to the head. With experience, you can practise this pose for ten minutes to experience its deeply calming effects (but see caution on page 101).

1 Take three blankets and fold them three times. Lie on your back over the neatly lined up edges of the blankets. Your head will be on the floor, and your shoulders on the blankets, about 5cm (2in) away from the edge.

2 Using minimum momentum and maximum abdominal strength, bring your legs and hips up in the air. Support your back with your hands. Adjust your position by squeezing your shoulder blades closer together so the upper part of your shoulders takes more weight and you can straighten upwards. Bring your elbows closer together. Stretch your legs up.

tip

If you feel a sense of exertion after coming out of the posture, lie for a few moments in Savasana (see pages 38–39) until your breathing returns to normal.

3 Keep your neck straight; never turn it from side to side. Although it might look as if the neck is taking a lot of weight, the neck muscles need to stay relatively soft. If possible, ask a friend to feel the muscles on either side of your neck to check they are not strained. Strain in the face means it's time to come down and rest. Build your time in the pose from one to ten minutes.

4 To come down, hinge at the hips and lower your feet a little over your head. Release your hands, and lower your legs with control. Lying flat, turn your head to the left and right a few times to release your neck. Move off the blankets and hug your knees to your chest and rock slowly from side to side. Lie quietly and feel the effects of the pose on your body. Matsyasana (see page 67) and a forward bend feel nice after Sarvangasana.

shoulderstand

against the wall

If you have trouble getting into a shoulderstand, this safe and controlled variation gives the same benefits.

1 Put three tri-folded blankets about 20–30cm (8–12in) away from the wall. Sit in front of them with your side and one hip touching the wall. Use your hands for support and ease yourself around to lean back on your elbows and bring your legs up the wall. Lift your head to ensure your body is straight. When you lie down, your shoulders should be 5cm (2in) away from the edge of the blankets and your head on the floor.

2 Bend your knees so that your feet are completely flat to the wall.

3 To lift your hips up, press your feet into the wall. Support your back with your hands. Open your groin to move your hips forward, lining up your hips and knees over your shoulders.

4 If you wish to go further, straighten your legs to bring your feet to the wall one by one. If you feel comfortable, bring your legs away from the wall one at a time. To come down, reverse the steps.

tip

For a steadier pose, hold the skin on your back rather than your clothes, which may slip.

! Shoulderstand and Halasana (see page 102) should be avoided in menstruation or in some ear and eye problems, e.g. detached retina or glaucoma. For heart problems, high blood pressure, previous neck injuries or pregnancy, seek professional advice.

halasana

plough pose

This upside-down forward bend soothes the nerves, and is a good ten-minute soother. It has the same effects and contraindications as a shoulderstand (see pages 98–101).

1 From a shoulderstand, lower your legs overhead. If your toes touch the floor, stretch your arms along the floor, and, if possible, interlace your fingers. Stretch your arms and legs in opposite directions. If your toes can't reach the floor, support your back with your hands. Build up to hold this pose for five minutes.

2 A more restful version is to roll back down slightly from the tops of your shoulders, widen and soften across your upper back, and lay your arms passively on the floor behind your head.

3 Slowly roll down to come out of Halasana. Use your abdominal muscles to lower both legs until you are lying flat. Rest for a while. Matsyasana (see page 67) is a complementary pose to do after Halasana.

sasankasana

hare pose

1 Get into child pose (see page 40): sit on your heels with your knees together. Fold forward over your thighs. Rest your forehead on the floor and drape your arms around you. Close your eyes and let go of any tension. Enjoy the reassuring massage of the belly pressing down into the thighs with each inhalation. For high blood pressure, or if your buttocks stay high in the air and you feel like you are nosediving, rest the forehead on folded blankets. Alternatively, stack your fists one on top of the other to rest your forehead on.

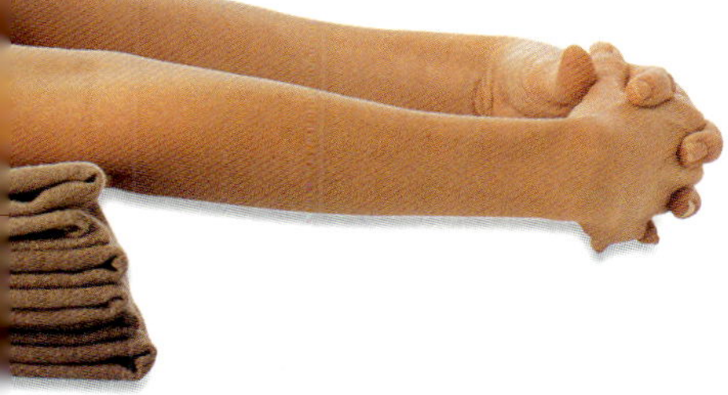

2 Hold the sides of your feet with your hands. Lifting the buttocks high, inhale and roll over your head onto the crown. On the exhalation, release back to child pose. Repeat five times.

halasana to paschimottanasana

If you are comfortable in a shoulderstand (see pages 98–101), follow on with this soothing pose. It has similar effects and contraindications.

1 From shoulderstand lower your legs overhead. You need to be careful not to overstretch the neck as you bring your toes to touch the floor. If you are not able to bring your toes to the floor, then rest them on a higher surface, such as a chair placed a couple of feet behind the head. (If your toes are not supported, then continue to support your back with your hands.)

2 Once your toes are resting on a surface, stretch your arms along the floor. This will help you roll more onto the tips of your shoulders and deeper into this upside-down forward bend. Interlace your fingers and deepen the pose by stretching your arms and legs in opposite directions. Build to holding Halasana for five minutes.

tip

If you are on a flat cushioned surface, then enliven the spine by rolling between these poses. As you do, maintain a relaxed back and shoulders. Slow it down to enjoy the feeling of massaging the muscles all the way along the spine and shoulders.

3 Roll out of the pose with control, using your abdominal muscles to lower both legs until you are lying flat. See shoulderstand (pages 98–101) for complementary asanas to follow on with.

9 Breathing

Breath, life and energy are all interconnected. Yogis have a single word for all three – *prana*. Energy points along the spine, known as *chakras*, serve as storehouses for the prana.

In yoga, breathing exercises known as *pranayama* are performed in order to increase the flow of prana through the body. Deep, conscious breathing is a powerful energizing tool. As more oxygen is distributed to the tissues, all cellular processes are enhanced so that the body is better able to repair damage, detoxify and combat disease.

Conscious breathing is a bridge between the nervous system, the mind and the feelings. It deepens understandings, increases clarity and calms the emotions. Spiritually, pranayama increases self-awareness towards the true goal of yoga – self-realization.

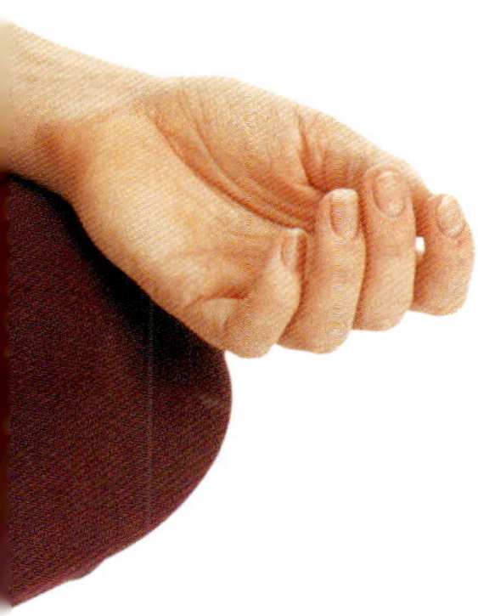

Ideally, you need to practise pranayama every day; a ten-minute session is enough to feel the effects. Pranayama can be practised on its own, or after asanas.

exploration: finding a comfortable position for *pranayama*

Some believe certain positions for pranayama and meditation are 'better' than others. But really, the best position is the one that is the steadiest and most comfortable for you, as long as it keeps the back, neck and head in a straight line. Any strain felt in the body will flow over to affect the breath adversely, so being comfortable is important.

The beauty of pranayama is that absolutely everyone can do it. The only requirement for practice is being able to breathe. If you are physically weak or ill, you can do pranayama lying down. Better still, bend your knees up and lean them in together. Take your feet wider than your hips, toes turned in. This position is supremely comfortable and you are less likely to fall asleep. If you feel yourself dozing off, separate the knees. If possible, try to practise pranayama for ten minutes every day.

Padmasana – Lotus Pose

A classical posture, where the legs are crossed and both feet sit soles up on the thighs, is advisable only if you have extremely flexible hips. When the hips are tight, the knees risk injury. Most westerners, who grow up sitting on chairs rather than sitting cross-legged on the floor, require dedicated hip opening work before they can sit comfortably in Padmasana. This posture is not used in this book.

Sukhasana – Comfortable Pose

Cross your ankles, then slide your feet apart so that each foot comes to rest underneath the opposite knee. To sit at length and remain comfortable in this position, your knees must be level with or lower than your hips. If your knees are much higher than your hips, or if you find your upper body tilting backwards, sit on as many folded blankets as you need.

Sitting on folded blankets helps to keep the back, neck and head in line.

Vajarasana – Firm Pose

Kneel with your knees and ankles together and sit down on your heels. As you bring your weight down, your inner ankles will tend to splay apart. Keep them as close together as possible. If you are on a hard surface, you may like to pad under the tops of your feet with a soft support.

Sitting on a Chair

Choose a chair that you won't sink down into. Sit erect with your shoulders in line over your hips, not leaning into the backrest. Shorter people can rest their feet on a support, such as a rolled blanket.

Experiment with a blanket folded several times to make a long pad laid across the knees. When you place your hands palms up on the blanket, your elbows will be more at right angles and the extra height brings softness to the palms. This roll can be used in any of the seated poses.

Swastikasana – Folded Leg Pose

From sitting, fold one leg in so your heel touches your perineum. Line up your other heel in front of the first one. Your knees will rest down towards the floor more easily than with Sukhasana, but you may still be more comfortable using a folded blanket to raise your seat.

ujjayi pranayama

The Ujjayi breath gives control over the flow of air into the lungs so that the breath becomes steadier, deeper and longer. More oxygen is made available, enhancing the purification and nourishment of each and every cell.

Ujjayi breathing is a little like drinking air through a straw. The glottis in the pharynx at the back of the mouth is partially closed. Friction is produced when air moves through the larynx, increasing the heat in the body. This allows the body to stretch very deep into the asanas, so Ujjayi is an ideal way to breathe during your yoga practice. Practice Ujjayi for 10 to 20 breaths while sitting. Take breaks when you need and finish with Savasana (see pages 38–39). As your comfort with Ujjayi grows, expand it for the duration of your practice.

tip

You should feel no stress as you breathe. Trying 'too hard' changes the lungs, diaphragm and nervous system, which in turn will adversely affect the rest of your body and mind. Evenness in the breath will lead to evenness of temperament. Mentally follow your exhalation its entire length. Don't allow your boredom to let you lose awareness of it. Don't let your impatience make you rush on to a new breath before the present one is fully exhaled.

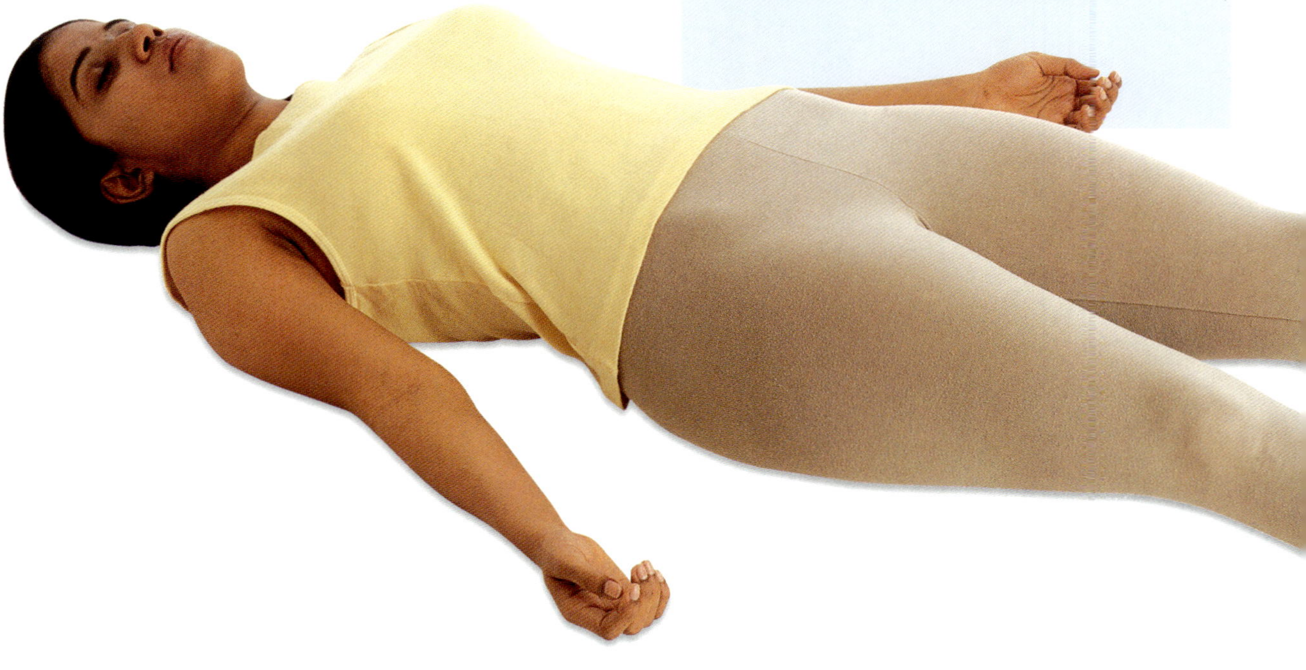

Ujjayi breathing will focus your mind and enhance your asana practice.

1 Sit comfortably and take several exhalations, each time making a long 'haaaa' sound through your mouth.

2 Close your mouth midway through the exhalation, but continue to make the 'haaaa' with your lips together. It will become a soft throaty sound that you can feel at the larynx. To check if you've got it, cover your ears with your palms and listen to the internal sound. It will have an ocean-like quality.

3 Now open your mouth again and make this 'haaaa' while breathing in. Close your mouth midway through again, to leave a soft friction in your throat. Once again, the sound will be like the ocean.

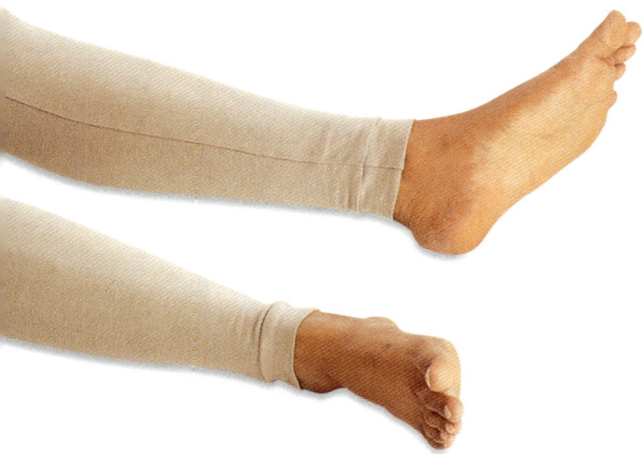

4 Continue the internal 'haaaa' as you inhale and exhale through your nose. It's not necessary to breathe loudly or aggressively. This breath is soft in nature and volume. While the sound produced will be audible to someone close by, it's not necessary to fill the whole room. The quality of the Ujjayi breathing is not measured in volume, but in length and steadiness. Bring your awareness to the constancy that this breath gives you. Each inhalation extends in a long, fluid way to deeply fill the lungs. Likewise, the flow of air through your nostrils is slow and steady for the entire duration of the out-breath.

nadi shodhana pranayama

alternate nostril breathing

Working on the physical, mental and spiritual levels, this is a valuable pranayama. It acts as a purification (*shodhana*) of the subtle energy meridians (*nadis*) and balances two important pranic pathways. As it helps balance the nervous system and calm the mind, it is a useful ten-minute exercise to do when you feel uptight.

As you inhale, observe the breath filling the lungs from bottom to top, right under the collar bones.

1 Sit comfortably with your eyes closed. Curl the index and middle fingers of your right hand into your palm.

2 Inhale fully through your nose. Close your right nostril with the thumb of your right hand and exhale fully through your left nostril.

3 Inhale through the left side. Close your left nostril with your third and little fingers, release your thumb and exhale through your right nostril, so that the air flows at a constant rate.

4 Inhale through the right side. Close your right nostril and open your left nostril to exhale.

5 Then inhale with your left nostril to exhale through the right. Each inhalation and exhalation keeps the flow of air through the nostrils at the same rate from beginning to end.

6 Inhale right, then exhale left. The rate of flow at the end of the exhalation should be the same as that at the beginning of the exhalation.

7 Inhale left, then exhale right.

8 Inhale right and finish with a final exhalation through the left nostril.

9 Lower your hand down and take as many easy breaths as you need. Observe the quiet stillness. When you feel ready, begin the next round.

Observe the stillness in the natural pause between the inhalation and the exhalation.

Each round contains three inhalations on each side, beginning and ending with an exhalation to the left side. To keep track, you can count with your thumb to your fingers on your left hand. Complete five rounds, resting your arm down, and taking as long as you need in between. Finish by relaxing in Savasana (see pages 38–39).

During the practice, keep your right elbow raised to avoid tilting your head to one side or placing pressure on your chest which impedes the filling of the lungs. Usually one nostril feels more open than the other. Nostril predominance shifts at regular intervals throughout the day.

tips

Practise alternate nostril breathing before bedtime to help you get off to sleep.

To help keep your breath steady, imagine there is a saucer of fine ash under your nose. If you inhale too greedily it will be sucked inside you. If you exhale too forcefully, it will end up all over your clothes.

deepen it

When you have practised this several times, implement a count. Inhale and exhale for a slow count of six beats each. When you become comfortable with this, increase it to eight. It should always feel natural, never tense. Force is always counterproductive in pranayama so if you find yourself straining, then reduce the count. Using a count makes the length of the inhalation and exhalation equal and gives a mental point of focus that can quieten the constant chatter of the mind.

The rate of airflow remains the same during the entire length of the exhalation.

10 Meditation and Therapeutic Yoga

Stilling the mind is not an easy task, and many people are put off meditation because they think they will not be able to do it. However, meditation can be practised by anyone. You do not have to be an expert in order to reap the benefits of this ancient practice, and even a short, ten-minute meditation can have a therapeutic effect.

Meditation and yoga bring a sense of relief, like coming home after a long and difficult journey. They help you develop greater perspective so that day-to-day worries can be transcended. Above all, they can show you that all obstacles are surmountable.

Don't be put off by any physical weaknesses. If you can't get comfortable on the floor to meditate, you can sit on a chair. If you find a yoga asana difficult to attain, your practice can be tailored to your needs. With the help of a specialist teacher, yoga can also be used therapeutically, to treat many common conditions.

five steps for *meditation*

Dedicate ten minutes a day to your meditation practice, and you will reap the physiological, mental and emotional rewards.

Relax Your Body

Yoga asana practice was originally designed to let the body sit comfortably in meditation. Short of a full asana practice, do a few stretches to increase your body awareness. Take a comfortable seated position with back, neck and head erect. (See the pranayama exploration, pages 108–109, for instructions on how to sit.) If it feels right for you, offer a personal prayer to begin the session. Sweep your mind over your body, systematically relaxing each part from bottom to top. You can also do Savasana (see pages 38–39) before sitting up to begin your meditation.

Once you have chosen your comfortable position, avoid further movement which will only act as a distraction. When you are sitting perfectly still, every physical sensation can feel like it is magnified. A small itch can become a huge torment. Breathe through these transitory sensations as they arise.

Relax Your Mind

Take three cleansing breaths by inhaling through the nose and exhaling through the mouth. Use a sigh as you exhale to release fatigue or tension. Now practise three rounds of Nadi Shodhana pranayama (see pages 112–113). Pay particular attention to the counting process. As with pranayama, strain is counterproductive to meditation. Keep the process relaxed.

Try out different sitting positions to find the one that is most comfortable for you.

Interiorization

The breath or a mantra are useful tools to increase your concentration. You could use the ancient sound 'Om' to help focus your mind. Begin by chanting this mantra aloud, change to whispering it, then finally repeat it only in your mind.

If instead you choose to use the breath as your aid, begin by observing the flow of air through the nostrils. The cool air flows in through the nose, and the warmer air flows out. In time, follow the cool inhaled air from the nose, to the trachea. Continue to observe without any hurry. Don't alter your breath, simply be aware of what is. Possibly you can follow the flow as far down as your bronchial tubes and the lungs. On each exhalation, observe the warmed air flowing out through the nostrils from inside the body.

Expand Your Consciousness

The mind has random thoughts, spreading over many subjects. Concentrating on a single object – the breath or a mantra – helps you to focus the mind. You can develop this practice further by concentrating on a single thought. Choose a subject on which you would like to expand your awareness, such as love or peace. The aim is not to prevent all thought, but to provide a focus point for the thoughts to revolve around. This one-pointed awareness is where meditation begins. Observe the flow of thoughts, like ripples in a lake, without following them. If you follow a thought that's not the focus of your meditation, you are lending it the energy to distract yourself. Practise mastery over the mind and gently bring your mind back to your chosen subject. The constant churning of the mind gives way to peace.

Closing Your Meditation

Guide your thoughts to a higher aim such as the realization of your true spiritual self. You might like to repeat a prayer at this point or to wish yourself and others well. Spiritual endeavours are of little use when not carried over into your day-to-day life. Let your peaceful feelings spill into your encounters with others.

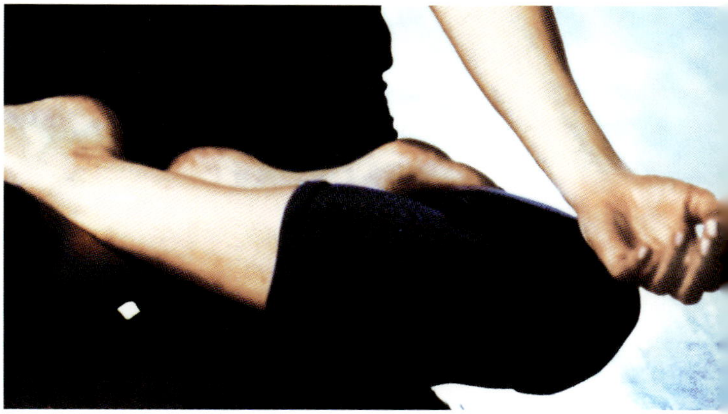

The benefits of meditation will spill over to your day-to-day life.

tips for Meditators

- Set aside a regular time to meditate. Traditionally the best times of day to meditate are sunrise, noon, sunset or midnight.
- If you feel daunted by the whole process, then commit to sitting quietly for ten minutes. During this time, just observe each thought, whatever comes, and let it go. You may find that after a minute or two, your mind is begging for something to think about. This is when you can give it your chosen meditation topic to contemplate.
- If you have a busy mind, 'doing nothing' and just observing in meditation might make you feel bored. If so, accept it and make boredom the subject of that meditation.
- Any action, performed with mindfulness, can be meditative. A walking meditation is useful if you find sitting for long periods is very uncomfortable, or if you tend to fall asleep. Keep your eyes unfocused, gazing down to the floor. Walk slowly in a circle with your awareness on the feet. Feel the sensations in each sole as it rolls down to contact the floor, bears weight and then peels off the floor to take the next step. After this walking meditation, sit and continue the meditation.

yogamudrasana

sealing pose

Yogamudrasana quietens the mind and is a good preparation pose for Savasana or meditation. You can add the hand *mudras* to your sitting position for meditation, and practise becoming absorbed in the breath (see page 117).

About Mudras

Mudras are gentle energy seals that are used to consolidate and strengthen the life-enhancing effects of yoga. Yogis believe that mudras serve to stimulate the flow of prana through the body and also to seal it in so that it's not lost or dispersed. Some mudras are similar to asanas. Others are hand gestures that may be used during pranayama or meditation. A number of mudras are linked with specific chakras.

Sit in Swastikasana (see page 109) by first folding your right leg in, then bringing the left heel in front of the right. Grasp your left wrist with your right hand behind your back. Inhale and extend the torso upward, then exhale and fold forward bringing your forehead to the floor. Rest for at least a minute, observing the breath and the mind. Then, with eyes closed, come up and change sides with the legs and hands before repeating.

For the mind to quieten you need to be physically comfortable. If this seated position does not feel steady and easy, then practise while sitting on the heels. Rest the forehead on a folded blanket if necessary.

Useful Mudras for Meditation

Mudras influence the subtle bodies and increase receptiveness to higher states of consciousness.

For *Gyana Mudra* (also called *Jnana Mudra*) join the tip of the thumb and index fingers while keeping the other fingers straight.

For *Bhairava Mudra* (Gesture of Shiva) place your right hand on your left. Rest your hands in your lap, with your palms facing up, and let the tips of your thumbs touch.

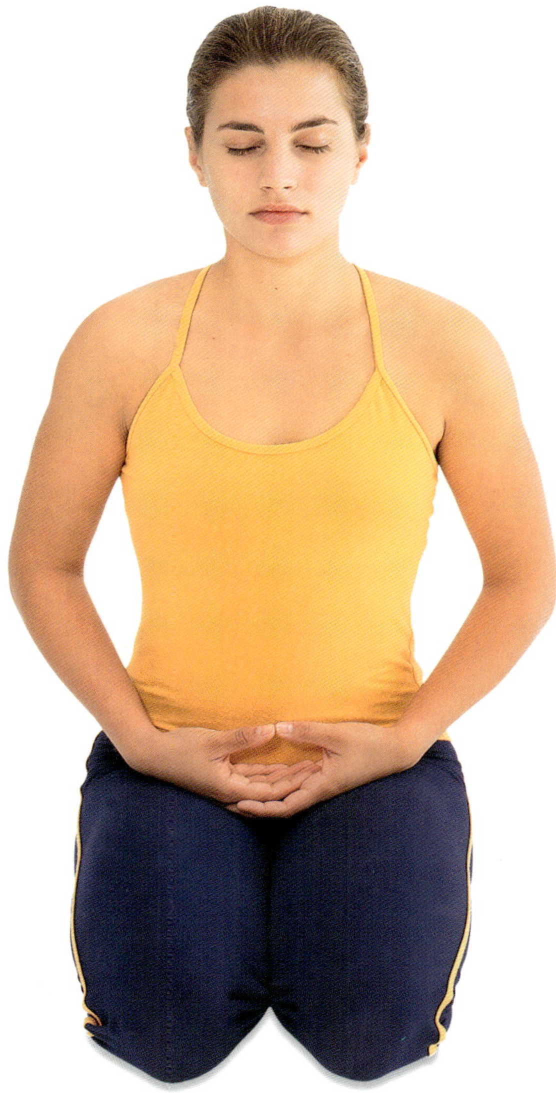

therapeutic *yoga*

Real health lies beyond the standard medical definition of 'the absence of disease'. True health encompasses a state of supreme well-being and vitality on the physical, mental and spiritual levels.

Yoga assists in the cure of diseases in a variety of ways. Each asana has specific structural and functional effects on the body. Yoga asanas promote the natural pulsations in the body. These rhythms assist circulation, increasing the vitality of each cell, tissue, organ and system.

Yoga helps to balance the hormonal and nervous systems. It balances the parasympathetic nervous system, involved in the 'restore and repair' response, to aid healing.

Learning deep relaxation is curative on many levels. Regular pranayama and meditation assist the mental and emotional response of the person to their disease.

Yoga as therapy for disease takes a holistic approach, considering each person as an individual. Indians consider each person has five *koshas*, or sheaths: physical, pranic, mental, intellectual and bliss. Ill-health results from a disharmony in the koshas which yoga helps to rebalance. Each of the following common practices – cleansing techniques, postures, breath work, meditation, analysis, experience, chanting, devotion and relaxation – promotes health through its actions on one or more of the koshas.

The table on pages 124–125 shows suggested asanas for common ailments. A holistic approach aims to correct the cause of a condition and this information is intended as a guide only, not as a substitute for advice from a qualified medical practitioner.

Yoga therapy is a holistic approach to rebalancing the mind and body.

ailments and *conditions*

Asanas work on specific parts of the body. When practised correctly, they encourage good health and prevent illness in these areas. Yoga practice can also be tailored to individual needs and used to treat specific complaints – this is yoga therapy, which needs to be done under the supervision of an experienced specialist teacher.

Regular relaxation and meditation help maintain mental and physical health.

common *ailments* and *conditions*

If you suffer from one or more of the following common ailments or conditions, it is important to consider the following advice or consult a qualified health practitioner before practising yoga.

anxiety Practise conscious breathing throughout the day to shift your thoughts from concerns and bring you back to the present. Physically work stress out with the asanas and perform them with as much mental focus as possible. After asanas, have a long Savasana and perform Nadi Shodhana pranayama.

arthritis If it is difficult to hold a pose, don't stay long in it. Develop mobility in the joints by moving in and out of the pose with easy flowing movements. Avoid moving into the pain; use props if necessary.

asthma Pranayama practice will retrain the breath. Back bends are useful as they lift and open the chest, encouraging fuller breathing. Avoid caving in the chest while practising forward bends.

constipation Find the cause. Check your intake of fluid and dietary fibre are adequate. Sun salutation, inversions and twists stimulate the digestive system and encourage elimination.

depression To help stay in the present moment, keep the eyes open during asana practice. Avoid forward bends as they can have the effect of making you more introspective.

diabetes Twists and back bends tone the pancreas. Yoga asanas increase circulation and overall vitality.

fatigue Rest mental fatigue with forward bends and savasana. Re-energize with pranayama.

herniated spinal disc Yoga can help slipped discs. Forward bending can seriously aggravate a slipped disc so hamstring flexibility needs to be developed and the back kept concave while bending forward. Support the area by strengthening the abdominal muscles.

hypertension Practise Savasana, pranayama and meditation. Practise inversions and back bends only under the guidance of an experienced yoga teacher.

immune support After asana practice, take extra time for Savasana and pranayama. Asana practice encourages health on the cellular level; Savasana greatly assists healing on a deep level.

insomnia Both mind and body rest more easily after being extended. Do energizing asanas like sun salutation and back bends in the mornings. If your practice is closer to bedtime, focus on forward bends and inversions. Take a long Savasana.

lower back strain Lower back pain has many causes and it is essential to get a correct diagnosis. While bending backward may alleviate one condition, it could aggravate another. Work with an experienced teacher to find what is appropriate.

menstrual disorders Back bends, forward bends, twists and sun salutation increase vitality to the pelvis. Inverted postures help balance hormones.

obesity Sun salutation helps burn energy. Practise plenty of standing poses, back bends and inversions.

pregnancy Yoga can assist pregnancy and labour. If you are new to yoga, do not begin yoga in the first trimester. Thereafter, attend a special prenatal yoga class to learn the necessary asana modifications.

stress Some stress can be worked out in the asanas. Concentrating on body awareness during practice gives a mental break from worrying. Long Savasana releases tension. Pranayama calms the nerves.

yoga during menstruation Inversions and strong twists and back bends should not be practised. Forward bends and relaxation are recommended.

yoga for the elderly The poses are likely to be less extended, but performing them with awareness will bring the same benefits. Flow into and out of poses, rather than holding them, to develop strength. Use props if necessary, e.g. hold the wall for balance.

therapeutic*yoga*

This chart shows which asanas are helpful for which conditions or ailments.

● Recommended
▲ Not recommended

	Awareness of breath p.20	Biralasana p.22	Surya namaskar p.28	Savasana p.38	Viparita karani p.41	Standing poses p.42
Anxiety	●	●		●		●
Arthritis	●	●				●
Asthma	●	●	●	●		
Constipation	●		●			
Depression			●			●
Diabetes	●					
Fatigue				●	●	
Herniated spinal disc	●					
Hypertension	●	●		●		
Immune support			●	●	●	
Insomnia			●	●	●	
Lower back strain	●	●		●		●
Menstrual disorders		●	●	●	●	
Obesity			●			●
Pregnancy	●	●				
Stress	●	●	●	●	●	●
Yoga during menstruation	●	●		●		
Yoga for the elderly	●	●		●	●	●

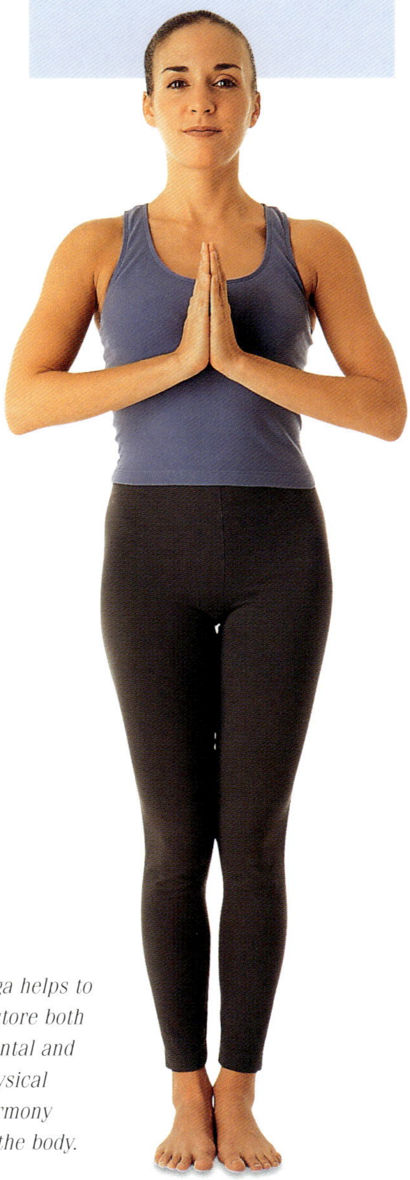

Yoga helps to restore both mental and physical harmony to the body.

	Bhujangasana p.62	Salabhasana p.64	Setu bandhasana p.66	Matsyasana p.67	Chakrasana p.68	Janu sirsasana p.77	Paschimottanasana p.78	Purvottanasana p.80	Baddha konasana p.81	Upavista konasana p.82	Sukhasana twist p.90	Marichyasana p.92	Jathara p.94	Sarvangasana p.98	Halasana p.102	Ujjayi p.110	Nadi shodhana p.112	Meditate p.116
	●	●	●		●						●			●		●	●	●
	●	●				●	●				●					●	●	●
	●		●			●	●	●						●		●	●	●
		●			●	●				●	●	●	●	●				
	●	●	●	●	●	▲	▲									●	●	▲
			●		●	●	●				●	●	●	●	●	●	●	●
						●	●		●	●				●	●	●	●	
	●	●	●								●	●					●	●
	▲		▲		▲	●	●										●	●
	●		●	●		●	●				●	●		●	●	●	●	●
						●	●		●	●				●	●		●	●
											●		●				●	●
			●	●	●	●	●	●	●	●	●	●		●	●	●	●	●
	●	●	●	●	●									●	●	●	●	●
						●			●	●								
	●	●	●	●	●	●	●			●				●	●	●	●	●
			▲		▲	●	●		●	●				▲	▲	●	●	●
	●	●	●			●	●			●	●			●		●	●	●

ten-minute posture pairs

Try pairing these postures for a revitalizing ten-minute yoga session. Perform the asanas with Ujjayi breathing (see page 110) and finish with a relaxation posture (see Chapter 3). To get the most from your practice, follow the guidelines on pages 18–19.

1 intense forward stretch (page 52) and...

...cat pose (page 22)

2 stomach strengthening twist (page 94) and...

...cow-face pose (page 84)

3 downward-facing dog (page 74) and...

...cobra pose (page 62)

4 shoulderstand (page 98) and...

...fish pose (page 67)

glossary

adho mukha svanasana downward-facing dog pose

ahimsa non-violence, fundamental element of yogic philosophy

asana yoga pose

baddha konasana cobbler's pose

balasana child pose

bhujangasana cobra pose

bhujapidasana arm pressure pose

chakra one of seven energy points along the spine, storehouses for prana

chakrasana wheel pose

chitta-vrtti fluctuations of the mind

garudasana eagle pose

gomukhasana cow-face pose

halasana plough pose

janu sirsasana head beyond the knee pose

jathara parivartanasana stomach-strengthening pose

kosha defence against disease

makrasana crocodile pose

mantra word or phrase repeated as an aid to meditation

marichyasana sage twist

matsyasana fish pose

nadi shodhana pranayama alternate nostril breathing

nadis subtle energy meridians

navasana boat pose

padmasana lotus pose

parsvakonasana side angle stretch

parsvottanasana chest to leg extension

paschimottanasana stretch on the body's west side

pavritta sukhasana cross-legged twist

perfect posture standing posture in which the body is balanced

prana the body's life force

pranayama breathing exercises used to increase the flow of prana

prasarita padottanasana wide leg stretch

purvottanasana stretch on the body's east side

salabhasana locust pose

samasthiti equal pose

sarvangasana shoulderstand

sasankasana hare pose

savasana corpse pose

setu bandhasana bridge pose

shodhana purification

sukhasana comfortable pose

surya namaskar sun salutation

swastikasana folded leg pose

trianga mukhaikapada paschimottanasana three-limbed forward bend

trikonasana triangle pose

ujjayi pranayama style of yogic breathing

upavista konasana seated wide angle pose

uttanasana intense forward stretch

vajarasana firm pranayama and meditation pose

vedas compilation of early Indian spiritual writings

viparita karani exercise that reverses circulation

virabhadrasana warrior pose

visualization meditation aid in which the postures are recreated in the mind

yogamudrasana sealing pose

yoga-sutra early yoga text

index